C000140965

Pub Strolls in
THE PEAK DISTRICT

Peter Fooks

COUNTRYSIDE BOOKS
NEWBURY BERKSHIRE

First published 2000
© Peter Fooks 2000
Reprinted 2003, 2007

All rights reserved.
No reproduction permitted without the prior
permission of the publisher:

COUNTRYSIDE BOOKS
3 Catherine Road
Newbury, Berkshire

To view our complete range of books,
please visit us at
www.countrysidebooks.co.uk

ISBN 1 85306 617 6

Designed by Graham Whiteman
Photographs by the author
Maps by Gelder design & mapping

Produced through MRM Associates Ltd., Reading
Printed by Cambridge University Press

Contents

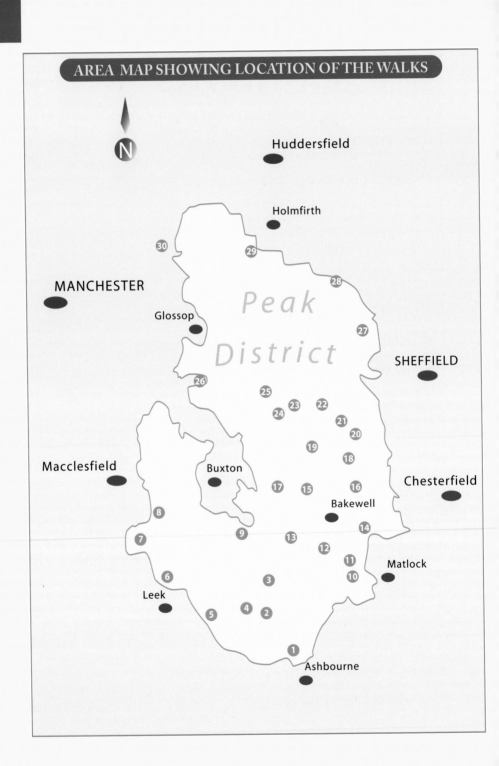

AREA MAP SHOWING LOCATION OF THE WALKS

N

Huddersfield

Holmfirth

30

29

28

MANCHESTER

Peak

Glossop

District

27

SHEFFIELD

26

25

23 22

24 21

20

Macclesfield

19

18

Buxton

17 15 16

Bakewell

Chesterfield

8

14

9

7

13

12

11

6

3

10

Matlock

Leek

5 4 2

1

Ashbourne

WALK

PUBLISHER'S NOTE

We hope that you obtain considerable enjoyment from this book; great care has been taken in its preparation. However, changes of landlord and actual pub closures are sadly not uncommon. Likewise, although at the time of publication all routes followed public rights of ways or permitted paths, diversion orders can be made and permissions withdrawn.

We cannot, of course, be held responsible for such diversion orders and any inaccuracies in the text which result from these or any other changes to the routes nor any damage which might result from walkers trespassing on private property. We are anxious though that all details covering the walks and the pubs are kept up to date and would therefore welcome information from readers which would be relevant to future editions.

The sketch maps accompanying each walk are not always to scale and are intended to guide you to the starting point and give a simple but accurate idea of the route to be taken. For those who like the benefit of detailed maps, we recommend that you arm yourself with the relevant Ordnance Survey map in the Outdoor Leisure series.

The Peak District, Britain's first National Park and the handiest for the greatest number of people, is popular with persons of all manner of backgrounds and tastes. Visitors to the stately homes of Chatsworth and Haddon Hall; motorists, cyclists and motor-cyclists on and off the Peakland roads; rock-gymnasts on the gritstone edges; hang-gliders on Rushup Edge – all these, and others, come here to indulge their chosen forms of recreation.

To those like me, there is only one way to fully appreciate all that the Peak District has to offer, and that is on foot; simply because there is no other way of reaching, and immersing oneself in, those hidden gems that make the district what it is – places like Lud's Church, Stanton Moor, Stoke Ford, Lathkill Dale.

Walkers themselves, of course, come in all shapes and sizes. This book is not aimed at, nor is it likely to appeal to the committed hill-walkers, scramblers and bog-trotters of this world; although one might hope that even they will find some choice nugget among this selection. Our target usership is primarily those who seldom if ever walk for enjoyment, but who nevertheless possess sufficient energy and enthusiasm to tackle an occasional short stroll in attractive surroundings; fortified, perhaps, with a tasty pub meal.

Peak District pubs are second to none. These thirty vary both in style and amenity. But all of them are friendly, welcoming country inns, and all provide excellent food and drink. Most – but not all – have their own car park and, unless the details here indicate otherwise, will not object to you leaving your car here while you 'stroll'; assuming, that is, that you are also using the pub's facilities. But do not take permission for granted; common courtesy demands that you ask first. Then again, if there is a public car park nearby, it is always preferable to use that one.

Most of the routes described here are accessible by public transport. Those without transport of their own are recommended to obtain a copy of the Peak District bus and train timetable, which is available at a very reasonable price from any Peak District Information Centre.

A walker's best friends are his/her feet. Pukka walking boots may not be absolutely necessary for these strolls, but they are ideal if you already have them. Otherwise, a good, sound pair of trainers, with suitable 'cleated' soles, should be adequate. If you want to walk in shorts, and if the conditions are suitable, feel free; but have regard to the possibility of overgrown footpaths, stinging nettles, and sheep ticks.

One or two of the strolls, where indicated, can be adapted for use with wheelchairs, but be prepared for uneven ground. The same applies with baby-buggies. As we found with our own kiddies, a papoose-style baby carrier is a godsend on country rambles, meaning you can take the smallest members of the family pretty well anywhere. Of course, once they are up off the floor, on their own two feet, you will be left standing!

Peter Fooks

Thorpe
The Dog and Partridge

DIRECTIONS TO START: TURN OFF THE A515 (BUXTON) ROAD JUST NORTH OF ASHBOURNE, FOLLOWING THE UNCLASSIFIED ROAD THROUGH TO THE TURNING FOR THORPE VILLAGE. THE DOG AND PARTRIDGE STANDS HERE ON THE CROSS ROADS.
PARKING: FREE PARKING IS AVAILABLE IN THE NARLOW LANE PUBLIC CAR PARK, DIAMETRICALLY OPPOSITE THE DOG AND PARTRIDGE (GR 164505).

To most tourists, Thorpe signifies Dovedale, the Stepping Stones and Thorpe Cloud. We used to come here by train, many years ago, when the local station, which was nowhere near the hill of that name, was also called Thorpe Cloud. Nowadays, the former station is merely a picnic site and car park on the Tissington Trail, a newer attraction which has taken the place of the once so popular transport facility, and which forms a significant element of today's stroll.

Our route starts with easy, level walking, mainly over quiet, unspoilt field paths, to Tissington, a particularly pretty estate village with a charming tradition. The return journey follows the former railway track, now totally ruralised.

The Dog and Partridge

This has been a justly popular watering hole for generations of walkers and day trippers. Most of the traffic heading for Dovedale passes the door of the Dog and Partridge, so its continuing popularity is never in doubt. The management, recognising the significance of the rambling fraternity in its success, is prepared to go to considerable lengths to encourage their patronage, for example by preparing, subject to prior arrangement, breakfast for long distance coach parties. An Avebury Taverns house, the opening hours, subject to adjustment out of season, are from 12 noon until 11 pm throughout the week, including Sundays. There is a full range of meals, bar snacks, jacket potatoes and sandwiches. All meals are prepared to order. Telephone: 01335 350235.

The Walk

Note: This walk can be adapted for the convenience of wheelchair users (and mums with baby buggies), by following Narlow Lane and Washbrook Lane in preference to the field paths.

① Starting from Narlow Lane car park and facing the pub, turn right along Spend Lane. Close to Pike House, turn right through a squeezer, following the waymarked Tissington footpath diagonally over the field. Continue over further fields to rejoin Narlow Lane by the entrance to Hollington End Farm.

② Cross the road, continuing around the field edge as waymarked, to Washbrook Lane, and turn right. Cross the main road

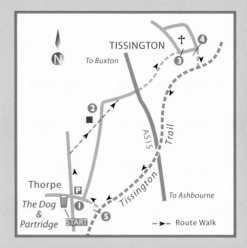

and enter Tissington Park, following The Avenue into Tissington village.

③ It will be worth your while exploring Tissington. A most charming estate village – the Fitzherberts have been Lords of the Manor since the 15th century and still occupy the hall – the sense of peace and gentility reflects the complete isolation of the village from the scourge of through traffic. There are mallards on the village pond, roadside lawns, a green – and five wells. Tissington is a delight throughout the year, but the ideal time to visit is during the few days immediately following Ascension Day, when all the wells (including a sixth 'Childrens Well') are dressed with beautifully decorated floral screens. Well-dressing is a widely observed custom throughout Derbyshire, but its true home is here in Tissington. The roots of the tradition lie away back in history. Some say it has pagan origins; others that it is a form of thanksgiving for the sparing of the village from the Black Death, or for the fact that the village's wells continued to run throughout the drought of 1615.

Tissington

④ Bear right opposite the village hall, following the former station approach road to reach the Tissington Trail. Pass through the picnic area and on. As you follow the broad, firm surface of the tree-lined trail, it is difficult to imagine that, within living memory, this delightful way was still a working railway. Those of us with longer memories may be excused a wave of nostalgia, while still delighting in the replacement.

⑤ Leave the trail at the former Thorpe Station, following the approach road back to Narlow Lane.

PLACES OF INTEREST NEARBY

Ilam Hall, a National Trust property west of Thorpe, is used as a Youth Hostel and not open to the public. The park and grounds are open, however, and admission is free (parking is Pay and Display) Facilities include guided walks, a shop and information centre and various educational aids. Telephone: 01335 350245.

Alstonefield
The George

DIRECTIONS TO START: FOLLOW THE A515 (ASHBOURNE TO BUXTON) ROAD, TURNING OFF WEST ABOUT 4 MILES SOUTH OF THE NEWHAVEN JUNCTION. DESCEND TO LODE MILL AND CONTINUE UPHILL TO ALSTONEFIELD. **PARKING:** THERE IS A PUBLIC CAR PARK (AND TOILETS) ON THE LEFT OF THE THROUGH ROAD, AT THE TOP END OF THE VILLAGE.

Alstonefield used to be a market town of some importance, standing at the junction of several roads and the centre of a large parish. Its stature has diminished over the years, but it remains an attractive upland village, with a welcoming inn overlooking its delightful greens with their widely spreading chestnut trees, and with a host of attractive footpaths, lanes and byways in the vicinity.

A walk of ups and downs – in the purely physical sense – takes us steeply down and up a couple of times, providing us with magnificent views. Not to mention the opportunity for rest, and possible refreshment, at nearby Milldale, a popular little hamlet which was familiar, in his day, to Izaak Walton.

The George

A 16th century former coaching inn, the George stands in the centre of the village overlooking a green, and is justly popular. You will find a cheerful atmosphere here, with quick and courteous service provided by obliging and friendly staff. The opening hours are from 11 am until 3 pm, and 6 pm till 11 pm in the week, with all-day opening on Saturday and Sunday. Food is available between the hours of 12 noon and 2 pm, and from 7 pm until 9.15 pm in the evening. The menu is varied and adequate, and the selection of puddings is a particularly mouthwatering speciality. Telephone: 01335 310205.

The Walk

① Turn right out of the car park, following the road round to the right and bearing left where the road forks. At the next junction turn left, and immediately left again, passing a cottage and following a walled lane. Where the lane bends right, keep straight forward through the squeezer and continue beside the field wall. There is a glorious view from here over the surrounding hills, with the Dovedale valley

Descending to Dale Bottom

recognisable over to the left. At the end of the field bear right through the gap, still following the wall, and descend steeply and carefully to Dale Bottom.

② Cross the road and continue ahead, climbing steadily along a walled way. From Grove Farm, at the top of the hill, the way continues as a metalled lane, to reach the hamlet of Stanshope.

③ Turn left at the road junction and, on the bend, sharp left again, onto a gravelled lane. After ¹/₄ mile or so, the lane is abandoned, as it bends to the right. Keep straight ahead here, following the field path for Milldale; initially on the right, and then the left, of the wall. After crossing several fields, the path enters a steep sided clough, descending more steeply. Some care is advised, particularly in wet conditions, when the underfoot limestone may be greasy. At the road, turn right for Milldale. There are toilets here, and the possibility of

light refreshments at the tiny village store. Not to mention the River Dove, with its beautiful little packhorse bridge – Izaak Walton's immortal 'Viator's Bridge'.

④ Turn aside by the shop, following this side lane (Millway Lane) steeply uphill. Although a metalled lane, you are unlikely to be bothered by passing traffic, so take your time. Pass Alstonefield's parish church of St Peter, continuing round to the right to reach the village, and the George.

PLACES OF INTEREST NEARBY

While in the area, there is no better way of filling an idle hour than by exploring the beauties of **Dovedale**. There are paths in either direction: either over Viator's Bridge and on towards Dove Holes and Ilam Rock; or north from Lode Mill towards Wolfscote and Beresford Dales. The best times – if you value relative solitude – are in midweek, or out of season. But with or without the crowds, it is a truly delightful area.

Hartington
The Devonshire Arms

DIRECTIONS TO START: VIA THE A515 (BUXTON TO ASHBOURNE) ROAD, TURNING OFF WEST ONTO THE B5054 JUST ½ MILE NORTH OF NEWHAVEN. **PARKING:** HARTINGTON TOWN SQUARE.

Hartington is an attractive, busy and popular small town, situated close to the middle stretch of the Dove valley, an area familiar to Charles Cotton, close friend and collaborator of Izaak Walton, who lived in the vicinity. The town has a goodly selection of shops, pubs and eating places – and the distinction, with the Leicestershire Vale of Belvoir, of being one of the only two places where genuine Stilton cheese can be produced.

Hartington Hall once played host to Bonnie Prince Charlie; needless to say, long before the YHA took over the premises!

Our gentle stroll beside the River Dove passes close to Charles Cotton's former home, providing a view of the spire-like rock in Pike Pool. The circle is completed by a saunter up and down the quiet local lanes, back to Hartington.

The Devonshire Arms

Situated in the very centre of Hartington, the Devonshire Arms is an attractive traditional 'Pubmasters' house offering fine ales and home-cooked food in congenial surroundings. Families are welcome, and so are well-behaved dogs. Food is served from noon until 2 pm and 7 pm until 9 pm during the week and from noon until 9 pm on Saturdays and Sundays. The menu includes such local specialities as Hartington Chicken, grilled rainbow trout and bilberry pie, and there is also a special children's menu and a vegetarian selection. The house has a function room, and overnight accommodation is available. Telephone: 01298 84232.

The Walk

① With your back to the Devonshire Arms, and the car park in front, turn left, following the road towards Hulme End. By the public conveniences, turn left, following the waymarked footpath (Peak and Northern signboard) for Beresford

Hartington

Dale. The opening stages of the path are gravelled and broad but, after crossing a narrow lane, revert to a pure, unadulterated – but well-signed – field path, which some may find preferable! After passing to the right of Pennilow, a small but attractive hill, the way descends to Morson Wood and the River Dove, in Beresford Dale.

② A footbridge leads over the river by Pike Pool, the charm of which is enhanced by a tall rock pinnacle. High above the river here on the Staffordshire bank was Beresford Hall, the home of Charles Cotton. Little remains of the the hall today, apart from a tower, and Cotton's Fishing House; both on private land. The river is recrossed at Beresford Lane, where a narrow wooden footbridge and a set of stepping stones vie for your favour. Continue now over a broad riverside meadow.

③ At the next footbridge, turn your back on the river, ascending a walled lane, which diminishes to a footpath. Turn right with the track, and left again at a metalled road.

④ Up the hill, turn left onto a waymarked farm track, bending right with the track and descending gently. Left again at a metalled road (Reynards Lane), back to Hartington. A footpath on the left, just before the village, saves little in the way of time, but adds variety.

PLACES OF INTEREST NEARBY

The Tissington Trail, once a light railway line running from Asbourne to Buxton, passes close by Hartington, to unite with the High Peak Trail at Parsley Hay station (GR 147637). At the station, the available facilities include car parking and cycle hire.

Wetton
Ye Olde Royal Oak

MAP: OUTDOOR LEISURE 24
(WHITE PEAK) (GR 109554)

WALK 4

DISTANCE: 3¾ MILES

DIRECTIONS TO START: FROM THE A515 (ASHBOURNE TO BUXTON ROAD) NORTH OF NEWHAVEN, FOLLOW THE THE B5054 THROUGH HARTINGTON TO HULME END. LEFT HERE, AS FOR ALSTONEFIELD, TURNING RIGHT AFTER ABOUT 2 MILES FOR WETTON VILLAGE. **PARKING:** PUBLIC CAR PARK AND TOILETS AT THE SOUTHERN END OF THE VILLAGE (GR 108551).

The directions for finding Wetton might suggest – not entirely accurately – that Wetton is remote from civilisation. A pleasant village on the high ground between the Dove and Manifold, it has some good 16th/17th century housing, a pleasant pub and an attractive church, not to mention a peaceful air. Man has been in this area for millennia; back at least as far as the time of Neanderthal man, who inhabited the limestone caves overlooking the Manifold valley.

A pleasant walk along ancient tracks and paths brings us to Thor's Cave, a vast and spectacular cavern high above the Manifold. Descending to the valley floor, we follow the route of a former railway to Wetton Mill (and the chance of refreshment) before returning over National Trust lands to Wetton village.

Ye Olde Royal Oak

An attractive, totally free house in the very centre of Wetton village, the Royal Oak is over 300 years old, and is especially noteworthy as the home of the World Toe-wrestling Championships – as seen, we are assured, on worldwide television. Our reception here was particularly warm and friendly but, to our profound relief, we were not invited to compete! The choice of liquor is astonishing. There were more than thirty single malt whiskies on offer when we called. Families are welcome, but dogs are restricted to the garden area. Opening times are from noon until 3 pm and between 7 pm and 11 pm, and home-cooked food is available between noon and 2 pm and from 7 pm until 9 pm in the evening. Specialities of the house include local smoked trout. And, if you go for the all-day breakfast, Staffordshire Oatcakes. Telephone: 01335 310287.

The Walk

① Starting from the pub, follow the road north-west, as signposted for Wetton Mill, bearing left with the road, past the church.

② Pass the 'Grinton' turning and take the next on the left, a rough lane and concessionary path signposted for Thor's Cave. At the far end of the lane, cross a stile on the right and continue along a clear field path. Over a wooden stile, the path branches. Take the right branch, descending carefully to reach Thor's Cave, a vast and impressive opening in the limestone crags high above the Manifold. For untold centuries a home of primitive man, the remains found here and in other

caves nearby include flint arrowheads, bronze bracelets and brooches, pottery – and, unlikely as it sounds, lion, hippopotamus and hyena bones.

③ Descend to the valley, still exercising care. Initially, the way is stepped, but this peters out to leave a steep, bare earthen slope which could be treacherous in wet conditions. At the bottom, turn right along the metalled roadway. This is not properly a road, but the now-surfaced track of the former Manifold Light Railway, for many years dedicated as a recreational route, and offering the relief of easy level walking after the descent from Thor's Cave. Continue along the track, crossing the Wetton to Butterton road, to reach Wetton Mill and a perfect excuse for a refreshment stop.

④ Follow the waymarked footpath route between the buildings, through the gate and up the hillside. Initially steep, the way levels off at a guidepost. Bear left here through a wooded area, soon joining a broad grassy glen leading up between steep hills.

17

Near Wetton

⑤ After passing through a gate, turn right through a squeezer opposite a house, waymarked for Wetton. Follow the wall round and up the hill, to reach a stile. Bear left now, over the field to a second stile, continuing ahead over the bank. Keep straight on now into Wetton, continuing forward along the village street to reach the Royal Oak.

PLACES OF INTEREST NEARBY

The Manifold Track, formerly the Leek and Manifold Light Railway, follows the river Manifold from Waterhouses (GR 084502) to Hulme End (GR 103593). The really energetic can follow the track through the valley – or hire a bike at Waterhouses to make the journey quicker.

Onecote
The Jervis Arms

MAP: OUTDOOR LEISURE 24
(WHITE PEAK) (GR 050552)

WALK 5

DISTANCE: 3 MILES

DIRECTIONS TO START: VIA THE A523 (ASHBOURNE TO LEEK ROAD), TURNING OFF AT BOTTOM HOUSE, OPPOSITE THE GREEN MAN, AND FOLLOWING THE B5053 FOR 2 MILES. **PARKING:** JERVIS ARMS' CUSTOMER CAR PARK.

A trim little village astride the River Hamps in the hilly Staffordshire Moorlands area, the name is pronounced 'On-cut'. This is one of the lesser-known parts of the Peak District, which is not to decry its appeal. There is no lack of enjoyable walking hereabouts, not least along the route of the former packhorse way to the Ecton copper mines. This walk, though, remains more local, with a straightforward saunter along either side of the River Hamps, and no climbing of any significance.

The Jervis Arms

This is a charming 17th century village inn with the River Hamps, spanned by a graceful footbridge, bustling through the garden area. Children are welcome here and there is a licensed family room as well as the riverside beer garden and non-smoking areas. The drinkables at the Jervis Arms include four guest ales, and the opening hours are from 12 noon until 3 pm on Monday to Saturday, evenings from 7 pm (6 pm on Saturday) until 11 pm. There is all-day opening on Sundays from noon until 10.30 pm. Home-cooked food, including vegetarian and children's meals, is served daily until one hour before closing. Telephone: 01538 304206.

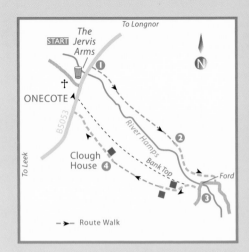

The Walk

① Start off by following the road north-east from the pub, crossing a stile on the right and following the waymarked footpath route over the fields. Keep upfield of the river for the driest ground; conditions can be a little damp, particularly during the monsoon season!

② Join a metalled farm road for a short

The River Hamps

Footbridge over the River Hamps, by the Jervis Arms

distance only, branching off left where the roadway bends right, to follow a rough lane and continue to the hamlet of Ford. Follow the roadway through a farmyard, turning right on reaching the public road.

③ Over the bridge, turn right onto a side lane, ignoring a footpath on the left here. Keep to the metalled roadway past Banktop Farm and continue to a second, modernised farmhouse. The way reverts here to a stone track, before crossing a stile and alternating between a green field way and an enclosed farm track.

④ At Clough House, the way reverts to a metalled road, continuing through to the road at Onecote. Turn right for the Jervis Arms.

PLACES OF INTEREST NEARBY

Blackbrook World of Birds, at Winkhill, south-east of Onecote, just off the A523. A lovely moorland setting is home to an amazing collection of wildlife. Facilities include a gift shop, information area, talks, displays and a picnic area. Telephone: 01538 308293 for details of opening times and charges.

Meerbrook
The Lazy Trout

<table>
<tr><td>MAP: OUTDOOR LEISURE 24
(WHITE PEAK) (GR 990608)</td><td>WALK 6</td><td>DISTANCE: 3¼ MILES</td></tr>
</table>

DIRECTIONS TO START: FOLLOW THE A53 (LEEK-BUXTON) ROAD, TURNING OFF WESTWARDS AT BLACKSHAW MOOR AND PASSING TITTESWORTH RESERVOIR. **PARKING:** LAZY TROUT CUSTOMER CAR PARK. THOSE NOT USING THE PUB ARE RECOMMENDED TO PARK AT TITTESWORTH RESERVOIR.

Buxton road came this way, crossing over via Windygates and passing through the gap between The Roaches and Hen Cloud before continuing over Goldsitch Moss to Flash and Buxton. There is little if anything remaining at Meerbrook today to remind us of this ancient trade route; just the church, the pub, a youth hostel – and a few cottages. But the attractive and popular Tittesworth Reservoir is close by, and there are splendid views of the Roaches and Hen Cloud to stir one's itchy feet. An easy walk, mostly along grassy field paths, allows us to enjoy those rugged views, without the necessity of actually scaling the heights!

The Lazy Trout

Families (and clean, dry, well-behaved dogs) are welcome at the Lazy Trout, an attractive building, with a family room among the facilities, standing on the village crossroads. The opening hours are from 11 am until 2.30 pm and 6 pm till 11 pm, Monday to Friday, with all-day opening from 11 am on Saturday and noon on Sunday. Bar meals and snacks are available throughout the week, both lunchtime and evening, and all dishes, in a comprehensive menu, are home-prepared. There is a good selection of home-made sweets, and daily specials are listed on the bar blackboard. Guest ales are also on offer. Telephone: 01538 300385.

The Walk

① Follow the side road (signposted for Roche Grange), turning right to follow a track past Lower Lee, and continuing over the fields in the general direction of the Roaches; a clearly identifiable rocky edge to

Hen Cloud

the east. The name translates as 'The Rocks'. Turn right on reaching another farm track, now with Hen Cloud – little brother to the Roaches – straight ahead. Continue to Frith Bottom Farm.

② Bear left at the far end of the yard, through a muddy gateway, and continue along the left of the hedge. Pass through a squeezer beside a field gate and guidepost and transfer to the right of the hedge, making for Roche House.

③ Approaching Roche House, cross a stile beside a guidepost, turning right and again heading towards Hen Cloud. Over a second stile by the farm, turn right, following the waymarked route over the fields.

④ As you approach Windygates Farm, bear right over the field to follow the wall round to a stile, continuing straight ahead then over two fields. At the end of the second field, cross the stile and turn left, following the waymarked 'Moorlands Walk' route. Continue over several fields, keeping a weather eye open for the orange discs which indicate the position of concealed stiles.

⑤ At the road turn right, back to Meerbrook.

PLACES OF INTEREST NEARBY

Tittesworth Reservoir has something for everyone, with fishing, a children's play area, refreshment facilities, visitor centre and nature trails. Or you can, if you prefer, simply recline, and moulder in idleness beside the lake!

The Roaches, from Lower Lee

Wincle
The Ship Inn

MAP: OUTDOOR LEISURE 24
(WHITE PEAK) (GR 962653)

WALK 7

DISTANCE: 5 MILES

DIRECTIONS TO START: APPROACHING FROM LEEK, FOLLOW THE MACCLESFIELD ROAD (A523). AFTER ABOUT 3 MILES, THE ROAD BENDS LEFT. KEEP STRAIGHT AHEAD HERE, TAKING THE UNCLASSIFIED ROAD. AFTER ½ MILE, TURN RIGHT, FOLLOWING MINOR ROADS, VIA DANEBRIDGE, TO WINCLE. **PARKING:** IF NOT VISITING THE PUB, LIMITED ROADSIDE PARKING SPACE CAN USUALLY BE FOUND ON THE CHESHIRE SIDE OF THE DANE BRIDGE.

Wincle is a remote and tiny scattered community close up to the Cheshire side of the border with Staffordshire, one of the loveliest and most romantic areas of the Peak District. The local river is the Dane, which flows down from Three Shire Heads through a glorious valley of rugged hills and woodland, beloved of generations of discerning walkers.

This walk at 5 miles is easily the longest in this collection. It is not necessarily the most strenuous; nor do I make any apology for the longer length. The pub – and the objective of the walk, one of the Peak District's outstanding curiosities – are too far apart to do it in less. A beautiful, yet quiet stroll, I met just one other walker on the entire circuit.

The Ship Inn

This fascinating, unspoilt, traditional village pub has a pair of foxes' heads glaring fiercely out over the cosy flagstoned snug from above the old-fashioned iron stove. A free house, the Ship is of indeterminate age, but it dates back at least as far as Jacobite days, when the landlord of the time was held up at gunpoint. Opening hours in the week (except Mondays) are from 12 noon until 3 pm and 7 pm to 11 pm. The same applies on Sundays, except that night-time closing is at 10.30 pm. Food is served from noon until 2 pm (2.30 pm at the weekend) and between 7 pm and 9 pm in the evening. Families are welcome; so are well-mannered dogs. All produce is fresh and the menu changes three times in the week, with Wednesday as fresh fish day – and the pub introduces 120 guest ales each year. Telephone: 01260 227217.

The Walk

① Cross the Dane Bridge and immediately turn left, following the waymarked riverside path for Gradbach and the Dane valley. An undulating path leads via alternating woodland and fields; sometimes wet underfoot, but always within sound of the river.

② Keep to the waymarked path as you pass Back Dane Farm, branching left at the next footpath sign. Pass a second farm and enter the Roaches Estate, continuing through the woods and ascending to a junction guidepost.

③ Turn right, ascending with the path

Lud's Church

and bearing left to reach a rocky outcrop, and the meeting point of several paths.

The Hanging Stone

④ Turn left along the ascending path to the left of a bridleway guidepost, looking out for a cleft on the right, the entrance to Lud's Church. Inside the cleft, steps descend to an impressive mossy-walled natural gorge. The name reflects the use of the gorge as a meeting place by Lollards, followers of John Wycliffe in the time of Richard II. 'Lud' is perhaps a corruption of the name of Walter de Ludank, who conducted services here in the 14th century. Return to the bridleway guidepost, continuing ahead along a good moorland path flanked by heather, bracken and bilberry, and with open views over the Dane valley.

⑤ Cross a stile, following the Swythamley bridleway. A concessionary path on the right here leads over the fields to the Hanging Stone, before descending to rejoin the main route. The name does not seem to have any macabre significance, but appears to refer to the stone's situation, hanging out over the hillside. Branch left by Hangingstone Farm onto a field path, crossing the fields and entering the woods. The path descends steeply and may be greasy underfoot, so take care. Cross a stile to rejoin the riverside path, turning left now, back to Dane Bridge.

PLACES OF INTEREST NEARBY

Rudyard Lake, south of Wincle, was built 200 years ago by James Brindley to feed the Trent and Mersey Canal. This delightful spot so enchanted one young couple that they became engaged here; and, in due course, named their son – who duly won fame as the poet and author Rudyard Kipling – after it. Attractions include a miniature railway, waterside walks with refreshments available in Rudyard village (GR 950583).

Wildboarclough
The Crag Inn

MAP: OUTDOOR LEISURE 24
(WHITE PEAK) (GR 982685)

WALK 8

DISTANCE: 2½ MILES OR 4 MILES

DIRECTIONS TO START: WILDBOARCLOUGH IS SITUATED WEST OF BUXTON ON THE UNCLASSIFIED ROAD LINKING THE A54 (CONGLETON) AND A537 (MACCLESFIELD) ROADS. **PARKING:** AT THE CRAG INN, OR, FOR NON-PATRONS, THERE IS A PUBLIC CAR PARK AT CLOUGH HOUSE, 1 MILE AWAY AT THE OPPOSITE END OF THE VILLAGE, BUT ON THE ROUTE OF THE WALK.

Wildboarclough is a charming little settlement set in a sylvan valley, deep in the heart of Macclesfield Forest and contrasting sharply with the wildness of the moorlands between here and Buxton. I came on it via a steep and narrow lane and was struck by its obvious 'Sleepy Hollow' character, a curious coincidence, bearing in mind the close proximity, just 2 or 3 miles away, of Wincle village. Tradition has it that the last wild boar in England met its death here. The local Crag Mill was at one time the site of the biggest post office in the country. And the village is dominated by one of the most attractive and alluring hills in the Peak District.

Shutlingsloe itself does not figure in the basic route (although anyone wishing to scale the heights may do so with our blessing!). For the rest, a straightforward walk, much of it along local lanes, but including a charming stretch of easy green track, will provide a pleasant stroll around the village precincts.

The Crag Inn

Families are welcome at the Crag Inn, a village hostelry with an attractive garden area and pleasant interior décor. Opening hours in the week are from noon until 3 pm and 7 pm to 11 pm; Sundays from noon until 5 pm only. The pub is closed on Mondays between November and March. Food is served daily from noon until 2 pm and in the evenings from 7 pm until 9 pm. There is no set menu, but the bar blackboards carry a mouthwatering selection of vittles to tempt the palate. When I was there, these included roast duck, steak and mushroom pie and half a roast chicken. There is a carvery on Friday evenings and on Sundays. Telephone: 01260 227239.

The Walk

Note: Apart from the option of ascending Shutlingsloe, the route can also be adapted for use with wheelchairs or baby buggies, by following the road throughout.

① Turn left from the Crag Inn, following the road for a short distance before turning off left at a waymarked farm track. This ascends, steeply at first, to reach a cattle grid.

② Cross the stile to the right of the grid (beside the farm gate), and follow the wallside track. Pass Shutlingsloe Farm and continue along a lovely green track. After passing a piece of woodland, cross a stile and bear right to meet the road. Continue forward.

③ Turn sharp right at the next road junction – or cut through the car park.

Keep straight on along this quiet road, climbing steadily. The gradient eases as you approach the outskirts of the village.

④ Bear right at Crag Hall, following the road round and passing the parish church, to reach the village and the Crag Inn.

Optional extension to Shutlingsloe: Any valiant souls wishing to ascend Shutlingsloe should divert at point 2 above, crossing the stile to the **left** of the cattle grid and continuing along the farm road. Before Banktop Farm, turn left beside the wall, following the waymarked route through the gap and continuing by the obvious path – steeper and more rocky in its upper reaches – to the summit (1659 ft).

There are very wide views from here over the surrounding hills and moors, and across the Cheshire plain. A viewfinder tablet set into the summit rocks points out the various landmarks to look for. This was placed here by the Peak and Northern Footpaths Society in memory of Arthur Smith: 'A doughty fighter for footpaths and access to mountains'.

Return to the cattle grid in reverse

Near Wildboarclough

order. Or, if you like, an easier though rather longer route drops down on the northern side of the hill, following a paved and stepped route and continuing for some distance beside the wall, towards the forest. Where the path crosses the wall, turn sharp right, following a fainter path and skirting around the hill, to rejoin the path of ascent by a 3-way guidepost.

PLACES OF INTEREST NEARBY
Macclesfield Forest, north-west of Wildboarclough, offers the opportunity to walk in the woods, beside reservoirs and to visit the popular Teggs Nose Country Park (GR 948723).

Earl Sterndale
The Quiet Woman

MAP OUTDOOR LEISURE 24 (WHITE PEAK)
(GR 090670)

WALK 9

DISTANCE: 3 MILES

DIRECTIONS TO START: LEAVE THE A515 AT BRIERLOW BAR, 2 MILES SOUTH-EAST OF BUXTON, FOLLOWING THE B5053 DUE SOUTH. TURN LEFT AFTER 1½ MILES FOR EARL STERNDALE. **PARKING:** THOSE NOT USING THE PUB SHOULD BE ABLE TO FIND ADEQUATE ROADSIDE SPACE.

The village of Earl Sterndale was an unlikely victim of the Luftwaffe, when an incendiary bomb, intended for an explosive dump in a local quarry, missed its target and hit, instead, the parish church. A quiet little village nonetheless, a main attraction hereabouts is the awe-inspiring reef hills of Chrome Hill and Parkhouse, guaranteed to stop the breath of every newcomer, on sight. Stunning views of both are the hallmark of this little walk in the Upper Dove valley. There is one short, steep ascent as we climb out of Dowel Dale; otherwise it is easy walking all the way, much of it along quiet country lanes.

The Quiet Woman

Said to commemorate 'Chattering Charteris', a nagging wife allegedly decapitated by her henpecked husband, the Quiet Woman is a plain, unvarnished traditional village tavern with cribbage tables and a tiled floor in the bar, and all manner of animals in the outer precincts. No meals are provided, but bar snacks are available most days, in the form of sandwiches and home-made pork pies. And stew in winter. Opening hours are from 12 noon until 3 pm, Monday to Friday, 12 noon until 4 pm at the weekend. Evenings from 7 pm till 11 pm except Sunday, when the pub closes at 10.30 pm. Telephone: 01298 83211.

The Dowall Dale Tearooms, at Dowall Hall Farm, halfway round the route, is the perfect spot to pause for refreshments. Clean and smart, with friendly service, parties are catered for. And muddy boots welcome! Telephone: 01298 83297.

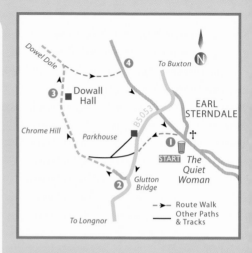

The Walk

① Follow the road north-ish from the pub. Past the last of the buildings on the left, go over a low stile beside a metal gate (no waymark here), crossing the field on a line to the left of the farm track. Pass an angle in the wall and continue through a gateway and on to a step-stile. Cross, and follow the descending path to reach the Glutton Dale road. Turn left.

Parkhouse Hill and Chrome Hill viewed from near Earl Sterndale

The entrance to Dowall Hall Farm

② Turn right at Glutton Bridge, continuing along the quiet, unfenced road beneath Parkhouse Hill, and enjoying the views of this one, and Chrome Hill. These remarkable hills are among the Peak District's eternal wonders with, despite their modest height, an almost alpine aspect. Reef hills, they originated, a yonk or two ago, at the bottom of the sea. Chrome Hill is open to the public – those of them with the stamina to challenge its steep slopes. Parkhouse, on the other hand, is private land. And if the author of this work has trespassed there, he ain't tellin'! Keep to the metalled lane, bearing right to cross the pass between Chrome Hill and Parkhouse, and continue to Dowall Hall, with its super little tearoom. There is a curious anomaly here. The farm is Dowall Hall while the dale, according to the Ordnance Survey map, is Dowel Dale.

③ Continue through Dowel Dale; not unlike the more familiar Winnats Pass, but on a smaller scale and without the traffic. As the road bends leftward, cross a stile on the right and follow the footpath up the hillside, continuing on over the fields.

④ Turn right at the road and continue across the B5053, back to Earl Sterndale.

PLACES OF INTEREST NEARBY

The spa town of Buxton, once fashionable as a health resort, has many attractions to offer the visitor: the Crescent, for instance, commissioned by the fifth Duke of Devonshire; the Thermal Baths, now converted into a shopping arcade; the former Pump Room, now housing a Micrarium. Then there is the Buxton Museum and Art Gallery, and the Pavilion Gardens. And the Market Place is claimed as the highest in England.

Winster

The Miners Standard

MAP: OUTDOOR LEISURE 24
(WHITE PEAK) (GR 238602)

WALK 10

DISTANCE: 2 MILES

DIRECTIONS TO START: A5012 TO GRANGEMILL, WEST OF CROMFORD; THENCE VIA THE B5056 FOR ABOUT 2 MILES. **PARKING:** MINERS STANDARD.

Winster is a small town of tremendous interest, with a long, strong lead mining tradition. The many fine historical buildings here include the National Trust maintained Market Hall, Winster Hall, the largest house in the village, and a 17th century Dower House. The area around Winster is still riddled with old mineshafts, most of them now capped and presenting no danger to the casual wayfarer.

This delightful short stroll follows ancient ways and crosses pleasant fields, to arrive at Winster village. A mildly strenuous ascent towards the end passes close by the rocky height that gives the place its name.

The Miners Standard

An attractive 17th century free house standing just outside the village and enjoying spectacular views over the surrounding hills. The name refers to the dish traditionally used by the miners for measuring the lead ore and, in keeping with the mining tradition, there are many reminders within the building of the district's links with the lead industry. There is some day to day variation in the opening hours, but patrons can be sure of a welcome within the period 12 noon until 3.30 pm and in the evenings from 6.30 pm until 10.30 pm. There is all-day opening on summer Sundays. Parties are welcome, by arrangement, outside regular opening hours. Home-cooked bar food is served from noon until 2.30 pm and between 7 pm and 9 pm in the evening. Children and well-mannered dogs are welcome. Overnight accommodation is available here and there are camping facilities. Telephone: 01629 650279.

The Walk

① Leaving the Miners Standard, turn right along the road, continuing round to the right at the turning for Elton and Newhaven.

② Turn right again on reaching a stony side lane. The guidepost on the junction carries the ram's head motif of the Limestone Way, but this lane is, in fact, very much older than that. The local name is Islington Lane, and it forms a section of the very ancient Old Portway, one of the oldest – if not THE oldest – of Derbyshire trade routes. You will search in vain for the village of Islington; but the name survives in the road itself. Follow Islington Lane for about ¹/₂ mile, ignoring a side turning – Lickpenny Lane – on the left.

③ Where the ancient track crosses a metalled lane, turn sharp right through a squeezer stile and continue diagonally over the field. Follow the fence-line in the next field, then bear right a little to reach, and cross, the B5056. Over the road continue, still on the diagonal line, through Oddo Park, to reach Winster via the churchyard.

④ Turn left via West Bank, then right again along the main village street, continuing as far as the ancient Market Hall. Turn right here, passing a side turning which will take you, if required, to the public conveniences. Otherwise, continue up the hill, climbing steeply around a double bend.

⑤ Near the last of the houses the gradient eases. By continuing ahead, it is only a short distance back to the B5056 and the Miners Standard. If, however, you still have a little breath to spare, turn left via a stile and follow the footpath as it climbs up the

Winster

field past the heavily wooded heights of Wyn's Tor. Continue beside the wall to reach a walled lane (the Limestone Way). A good spot this to pause awhile and recover your breath – and to enjoy the pleasing prospect of Central Derbyshire's hills and dales before following the track down to the road, and back to the Miners Standard.

PLACES OF INTEREST NEARBY

Being something of an old cynic, I have always maintained that **Matlock Bath** is a good place to walk out of. So it is, of course. But Derbyshire's Little Switzerland does have a lot to commend it to the visitor. Matlock Bath railway station is today the home of the Derbyshire Wildlife Centre. The cable cars leave here too, for the Heights of Abraham Pleasure Gardens and the Victoria Prospect Tower.

Birchover
The Druid

MAP: OUTDOOR LEISURE 24
(WHITE PEAK) (GR 236621)

WALK 11

DISTANCE: 2¾ MILES

DIRECTIONS TO START: A5012 TO GRANGEMILL, WEST OF CROMFORD; THENCE VIA THE B5056 FOR ABOUT 3 MILES TO A TURNING ON THE RIGHT, LEADING DIRECTLY INTO BIRCHOVER VILLAGE. **PARKING:** USE OF THE PUB CAR PARK IS RESERVED FOR THOSE BOOKING A MEAL, BUT ADEQUATE ROADSIDE PARKING SPACE IS AVAILABLE IN THE VICINITY.

The area around Birchover is one of the most fascinating locations in the Peak District. The village's more recent history is as a stone quarrying community. But man has been around here for many thousands of years, with the Stanton Moor area being particularly rich in reminders of his passage.

One of the oldest Peakland roads – the Old Portway – passes nearby, overlooked by a medieval hermitage and impressive rock formations. This gentle, easy walk explores the Stanton Moor plateau, viewing the evidence of primitive man's habitation.

The Druid

An attractive and popular free house dating back over 200 years and reflecting, in its name, the district's prehistoric heritage. The opening hours throughout the week, are from 12 noon until 2 pm and 7 pm to 9 pm. This is primarily a restaurant and the range of food on offer, both on the printed menu and on the daily specials board, is staggering in its diversity. Telephone: 01629 650302.

The Secret Garden, on The Green, provides an excellent pot of tea (but not on a Wednesday).

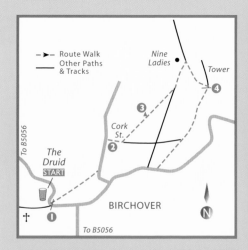

The Walk

① On the bend of the road, directly opposite the pub entrance, a wooded footpath will be seen ascending steeply. Follow this as it climbs, above and to the north of Main Street. Turn left at Birchover Road, walking towards Stanton in Peak.

② On the brow of the hill turn right, joining the waymarked path, to reach and cross a stile giving access to Stanton Moor. As moorland goes, Stanton is one of the gentler and more visitor friendly areas. There is heather here, and bilberries in season, and sandy ways; but nothing in the nature of bogs. And there is abiding evidence of the colonisation of the moor, extending back as far as the Bronze and New Stone Ages. The first curiosity met along the way is the Cork Stone, a great upright stone with footholds and iron handholds, standing beside the footpath. Ascend it if you dare – or can; the footholds are badly eroded. Turn left at the Cork Stone, following a clear path to the right of a small abandoned quarry area and bearing

right where the way branches, to reach the summit of the moor (1060 ft). There are one or two conveniently placed rocks here where you can rest awhile and enjoy the all round views.

③ Continue over the moor to join the main north/south track. A sandy way today, it is difficult to appreciate that this track is probably all of four thousand years old. This brings us to the 'Nine Ladies', an ancient stone circle which, together with the nearby 'King Stone' is reputed to have been a group of ladies, and their fiddler, punished for dancing on the Sabbath. Opposite the Nine Ladies, turn right onto a side path, crossing the moor to reach the Reform Tower, built to commemorate the passing of Earl Grey's Reform Bill in 1832. Cross the stile and descend carefully to join the perimeter path turning right.

④ Following the path south, a side track will be seen on the left. This leads to the Cat Stone, a similar feature to the Cork Stone, largely hidden among the encroaching trees. Rejoin the perimeter path and continue. There are more good

The Cork Stone

views here over the Derwent valley. Landmarks to look for include the unmissable industrial complex down below on the site of the former Millclose Mine. In the distance, the hilltop block of Riber Castle. And, perhaps, the Sherwood Foresters' memorial lighthouse on Crich Stand. As you proceed, look out for the flat 'Gorse' (or Gorsedd) stone, on the rim of the moor, before descending to join Lees Road. Turn right now, following the road back to Birchover.

PLACES OF INTEREST NEARBY

One of the finest historical buildings in the Peak District, **Haddon Hall**, on the A6 between Bakewell and Rowsley, has been in the Duke of Rutland's family for over 800 years. The descendants of William the Conqueror's natural son Peveril held the estate for 100 years before it passed to the Vernons. The house then passed to the Manners family – later the Dukes of Rutland – by marriage in the 16th century. Little has been added since the days of Henry VIII and no other medieval house has so triumphantly withstood the passage of time. Particularly attractive features include the magnificent Great Hall and the beautiful terraced Rose Garden. For fuller details, including entrance charges and opening arrangements, telephone: 01629 812855.

Youlgreave
The Farmyard

DIRECTIONS TO START: FROM HADDON, ON THE A6, FOLLOW THE B5056 AND UNCLASSIFIED ROADS TO ALPORT AND YOULGREAVE. THE FARMYARD INN IS AT THE WESTERN END OF MAIN STREET. **PARKING:** FARMYARD INN CAR PARK. ON STREET PARKING, FOR NON-PATRONS, COULD POSE PROBLEMS.

Youlgreave is a charming old hilltop village high above the rivers Lathkill and Bradford, which appears to have developed haphazardly, such is the higgledy-piggledy nature of its narrow roads and lanes. The local Youth Hostel was formerly the Co-op store, and the original trade signs are still prominently displayed on the frontage. But the pride of the village is its splendid church, a landmark for miles around and one of the finest in the Peak District. Parts of the building, and many of the items within, date back to the 12th century. A quaint tradition in former years concerned the practice whereby local farmers were allowed to take their dogs into church. Any cases of misbehaviour resulted in the offending animals being whipped off the premises.

A gentle circular meander, this stroll takes us along the banks of two of Peakland's most charming rivers: the Bradford and the Lathkill.

The Farmyard

Parts of the Farmyard date back over three centuries, at which time it was, indeed, a farm. A free house, it was converted into an inn in 1829 and is claimed to be the only 'Farmyard Inn' in England. The bar room, especially, has a particularly pleasing old-world atmosphere with its big open fireplace and old beamed ceilings. A closer look at the building as a whole indicates that it has been modernised, but tastefully. The pub is open all day from 12 noon Saturday and Sunday but only from 5 pm onwards Monday to Friday. Food is served lunchtime and evening at the weekend and in the evenings Monday to Friday. Telephone: 01629 636221.

The Meadow Cottage Tearooms, at the foot of Holywell Lane, are also highly recommended.

The Walk

① Follow Main Street towards the village centre, turning right into Holywell Lane and descending to Bradford Dale.

② Turn left through a squeezer, at the foot of the hill, following the river through

Bradford Dale

the dale. Sections of the Bradford tend to dry out at times, but a series of ponds, a legacy of the days when the river powered a local cornmill, continue to provide an arena for the ubiquitous ducks. Cross Mawstone Lane, continuing along a rough track and the occasional footpath and still following the River Bradford, to Alport.

③ Cross the road, joining and following the River Lathkill upstream. Lathkill Dale is one of the Peak District's most beautiful valleys, the river flowing through a wealth of differing scenery, from narrow limestone gorges to broad, green meadows. This lower stretch is particularly delightful – a lovely meadowland path giving pleasant, easy walking from Alport to Conksbury Bridge.

④ By Coalpit Bridge – the name recalls the former use of the crossing by packhorse trains from the mines around Chesterfield – turn left up a narrow lane, passing Raper Lodge. Turn left at the road, continuing into Youlgreave; then right by the church, back to the Farmyard Inn.

PLACES OF INTEREST NEARBY

Arbor Low, about 3 miles west of Youlgreave (GR 160636), sometimes called the Derbyshire Stonehenge, is the third largest stone circle in England and dates back about four thousand years, to the late Neolithic or early Bronze Age. Unlike Stonehenge, the stones at Arbor Low are recumbent – and may be considered less impressive. But they are no less worth visiting on that account. Their high, bleak and open situation alone adds drama to the scene.

Raper Lodge, Lathkill Dale

Monyash
The Bull's Head

DIRECTIONS TO START: MONYASH IS 5 MILES WEST OF BAKEWELL TOWN CENTRE, ON THE B5055. **PARKING:** THE BULL'S HEAD.

The village of Monyash was a regional centre of the lead mining industry, and it was here that the Barmote used to sit to sort out mining disputes. Ropes and candles were made here too, and quarrying also provided employment. The village lies at the head of Lathkill Dale, one of the Peak District's most entrancing valleys.

This easy and relaxing short stroll provides a brief introduction to the delights of upper Lathkill Dale, tempting the newcomer to explore further. But that must wait for another day, as we saunter over higher ground, along well-trodden ways, back to Monyash.

The Bull's Head

Ornate iron stanchions support the beamed ceiling of this fine old village pub, and an imposing coat of arms decorates the wall above the stone-built fireplace with its wintertime coal fire. This is a free house, offering traditional home-cooking and real ales in comfortable surroundings. Families are welcome, as also are clean, well-behaved dogs. Facilities include a pool room, and the outside drinking area overlooks the village green. Lunchtime opening, from Monday to Friday, is from 12 noon until 3 pm and evening opening from 7 pm. The pub is open all day at the weekend and on bank holidays in summer. Food is served from 12 noon until 2 pm (2.30 pm at the weekend) and in the evening from 7 pm until 9 pm except on Saturday when serving hours are from 6.30 pm until 9.30 pm. Telephone: 01629 812372.

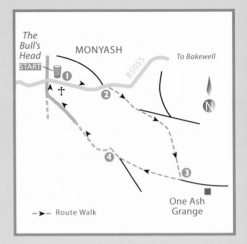

The Walk

① Walk eastwards through the village, continuing on along the road to the foot of the hill.

② Leave the road here, entering the broad upper section of Lathkill Dale. In the third field, leave the dale, crossing a stile beside a gate and ascending gently alongside the wall, with the rocky 'gulch' of Lathkill Dale visible below on your left. Bear right with the track, leaving the wall and continuing over the fields for ½ mile, after which the way branches left and right. Ignore the leftward track, which passes through the gateway and leads to One Ash Grange, once a penitentiary centre for recalcitrant

Lathkill Dale

Monyash

monks. There must have been worse places to serve out a sentence!

③ Turn right (approximately west), again following the wall on your left. Cross to the left of the wall and continue over dry, shallow Fern Dale. Recross the wall and turn left, joining a narrow walled lane.

④ Follow the lane back to Monyash, passing the village pond and continuing to the Bull's Head.

PLACES OF INTEREST NEARBY
Magpie Mine, north of Monyash near Sheldon is one of the best-preserved lead mines in the Peak District. Said to have been worked for over 300 years, and with a 728 foot main shaft, there is a lot of superstition attached to Magpie Mine, with talk of curses, ghosts, flood, fire and roof falls. The surface works have been restored as a visitor attraction, and are accessible by field-path.

Beeley
The Devonshire Arms

MAP: OUTDOOR LEISURE 24 (WHITE PEAK) (GR 266674)	WALK 14	DISTANCE: 3¾ MILES

DIRECTIONS TO START: LEAVE THE A6 AT ROWSLEY, TRAVELLING NORTH ON THE B6012 FOR JUST OVER A MILE. **PARKING:** AT THE DEVONSHIRE ARMS.

Although a very ancient settlement which was mentioned in the Domesday Book, Beeley is one of those blessed places which is passed, in season, by swarms of tourists, but is seldom invaded by the hordes. A quiet and pretty village, where traditional 17th century buildings blend with 19th century estate properties, the frontage to the Chatsworth road is so brief that the mass of visitors is past in the twinkling of an eye,

doubtless without even recognising its existence. And long may it be so.

For ourselves, a gem of a walk takes us gently uphill beside the Beeley Brook and through delightful woodlands, to the interestingly named 'Hell Bank Plantation'. A stony descent follows to Beeley Hilltop, from where a delightful and well-trodden field path leads back to Beeley village.

The Devonshire Arms

A picturesque, clean and attractive free house, the Devonshire Arms was formerly three separate cottages before its conversion, in 1747, to a coaching inn. It counts among its former patrons the writer Charles Dickens – and King Edward VII in the course of his extra-marital adventures. Families – including the children – are always welcome, as are guide dogs. Opening hours are from 11 am to 11 pm on Monday to Saturday and noon until 10.30 pm on Sundays. Bar meals are served every day from noon until 9.30 pm and special dishes of the day are always available in addition to the regular menu. Specialities include Friday Fish Night and, subject to advance booking, a Sunday Victorian Breakfast. Telephone: 01629 733259.

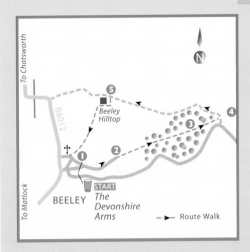

The Walk

① Leaving the Devonshire Arms, follow the adjacent minor road out of the village, keeping the Beeley Brook on your right. Ignore a little footbridge (a waymarked footpath) on the right and continue left with the road; then immediately right again into a broader way. This diminishes in

Beeley

Beeley Hilltop

width as it proceeds, eventually slimming down to a farm lane.

② Leave the lane, following the way-marked footpath on the left. Where the way branches, take the rightward option, passing through a gate and continuing on a delightful woodland path, always with the brook in close proximity. Cross the brook and continue, climbing steadily.

③ Turn sharp left at a junction of paths; then right again at a second junction, still climbing, to reach a stile leading out to a stony track close to Beeley Lane.

④ Turn left along the walled track. A gentle descent follows, initially with woodland on the left and the open moor on the right. As the woods end, the view opens out, with glorious prospects over the Derwent valley.

⑤ At the nearside of Beeley Hilltop

Farm, turn left through a squeezer, following the line indicated by the adjacent guidepost. Join the farm track and follow round to the right, keeping straight ahead at a junction to reach a gate, and continue along the right-hand side of the field wall. Once over the hilltop, Beeley comes into view ahead, giving a clear guide as to the direction to follow – via a well-used path with good waymarking all the way.

PLACES OF INTEREST NEARBY

Chatsworth House, the 17th century Palladian home of the Duke and Duchess of Devonshire, is one of the grandest stately homes in England. There are extensive ornamental grounds, features of which include the magnificent Emperor Fountain. The parkland, which is open to the public, was designed by Capability Brown. The house and garden, farmyard and adventure playground are open daily between Easter and the end of October. For detailed information, including hours and admission charges, telephone: 01246 565300.

Little Longstone
The Packhorse

MAP: OUTDOOR LEISURE 24 (WHITE PEAK) (GR 190717)	WALK 15	DISTANCE: 3½ MILES

DIRECTIONS TO START: FROM ASHFORD IN THE WATER VILLAGE, JUST OFF THE A6, FOLLOW GREAVES LANE AND THE B6465 TO MONSAL HEAD. **PARKING:** MONSAL HEAD (PAY AND DISPLAY, GR 185715).

Little Longstone is, as its name suggests, a small village, linear in form and just – but only just – off the beaten track. Although situated close to the ancient Portway route and to the ever-popular Monsal Head, it remains, for much of the time, blessedly quiet. Apart from the visitors' cars, that is, which, on busy days, tend to overflow along the road from the said Monsal Head. A major attraction at the Head itself is the Monsal Dale Viaduct. When the viaduct was built, the great John Ruskin condemned this intrusion on the beautiful vale, in no uncertain terms. A hundred years later, after the railway line was closed, there was a proposal to demolish the viaduct. But it had, by then, become an established, essential and much admired element of the scenery, and the resulting protests put paid to the idea!

Our stroll begins at Monsal Head, from where a short road walk leads to Little Longstone and the ancient Packhorse inn. From here, parkland and field paths are followed to the outskirts of Ashford. An easy network of walled lanes brings us back to the rim of Monsal Dale.

The Packhorse

Originally built as a pair of lead-miners' cottages in the early 17th century, the Packhorse has been a pub since the 1780s. It remains unspoilt, with no juke box, TV or fruit machine. A Marston's house, lunchtime opening is from 11.30am to 3pm in the week and 12 noon until 3pm on Sundays. Evenings from 5pm till 11pm on Monday to Friday, 6pm till 11pm on Saturday and 7pm to 10.30pm on Sundays. There is a full range of meals and bar snacks, and specialities of the house include Packhorse Pie (named after the pub, not the contents), Steak and Stilton Pie and lamb steak with redcurrant and rosemary. Not to mention the daily specials board. All food is prepared from fresh ingredients. Telephone: 01629 640471.

The Walk

① Starting from the Monsal Head car park, cross the road and follow the side lane to Little Longstone and the Packhorse.

② A little way beyond the pub, turn right at a guidepost. There are two routes waymarked here; take that at right-angles to the road – the Ashford and Monsal Trail path – over parkland. Cross the route of the Bakewell to Buxton railway line, now converted to a recreational route. Continue over fields, crossing Longstone Lane.

③ Continuing forward, pass a farm and descend to an enclosed pathway beside a barn. Cross a second lane and one further field, turning left then towards Ashford.

④ At the top of the rise, and opposite Highfield Farm, turn right into an unmetalled farm lane (Pennyunk Lane). The way descends gently, passing Ploverfield cottage and bending sharp right. Where the track enters a field and terminates, turn left alongside the wall and continue to the top of the field. Cross the stile and turn right, entering another walled lane and continuing to the brink of Monsal Dale.

⑤ The route back to Monsal Head from here is straightforward. But first, if nobody has beaten you to it, you may wish to take advantage of the seat here for a five-minute break while you rest your weary limbs and enjoy the view over the dale. Alternatively, you could stretch out on the grass, for the same purpose. Sadly, the view of the viaduct is not quite as I remember it from some years ago, due to the increased growth of trees on the intervening slopes of the dale. Looking to your left here, take note of the hill overlooking this side of the dale. This is Fin Cop, the summit of which was the site of a prehistoric hill fort. Lower down the same slope, closer to the River Wye, you may be able to pick out the site of

Pennyunk Lane

Hob's House – not a house at all, but a weird assemblage of rocks with a certain unsavoury reputation. Like Fin Cop, this is on private land; but my own youngsters trespassed there, on an expedition some years ago and detected a distinct eeriness about the place.

PLACES OF INTEREST NEARBY

Bakewell is the headquarters town of the Peak District National Park; and, indeed, the only true town within the Park. A busy and popular place, buildings of interest include the church and the old Market House, now housing the Information Centre. There is still a regular stock market held here, as well as the annual Bakewell Show. Bakewell is also a popular shopping centre and particularly noteworthy shops include the Bakewell Pudding Shop and one or two excellent bookstores.

Baslow
The Rutland Arms

DIRECTIONS TO START: APPROACHING FROM CHESTERFIELD ON THE A619, ENTER BASLOW, KEEPING RIGHT AT THE NEXT ROUNDABOUT. THE RUTLAND ARMS IS ON THE BEND, BY THE PARISH CHURCH. **PARKING:** AT THE RUTLAND ARMS.

Baslow is one of those attractive villages which, all too often, we tend to pass through en route for pleasures elsewhere. Perplexingly, it consists of four ends. Far End, on the Sheffield road, is little more than a clutch of farms, while Over End, where most of the people live, is 'up the hill' from the main road. Nether End is the best-known to visitors, providing an access point to the Chatsworth Estate, a busy car park and toilets and some super walking on the gritstone edges. The old village is at Bridge End. The church is here, as well as two excellent pubs and an ancient bridge with a tiny integral toll booth.

Our walk begins at this bridge: an enjoyable blend of quiet lanes, pastoral paths and woodland ways. The distance of 4 miles can be reduced to 3½ – but the full mileage is recommended.

The Rutland Arms

A Mansfield house serving CAMRA approved real ales, the Rutland Arms stands on the Calver road, alongside the medieval bridge which formed the original crossing of the River Derwent. The inn claims to have its own resident ghost – more accurately described, perhaps, as a 'presence', which is sensed in passing, rather than seen. The landlord assures me that it is quite harmless. Winter opening hours are from 12 noon until 3 pm (4 pm on Saturdays), with evening opening from 6 pm till 11 pm on Monday to Saturday and 7 pm to 10.30 pm on Sundays. There is all-day opening in summer. Food is served every day, lunchtime and evening, and there is a full range of regular items and daily specials, including vegetarian dishes, seafood, grills, children's meals and sweets. Not to mention sandwiches and jacket potatoes. Families are welcome, and guide dogs, and overnight accommodation is available. Telephone 01246 582276.

The Walk

Note: The total distance of 4 miles can be reduced to 3½ by following Bramley Lane between points 3 and 5, thus omitting the northernmost piece of the walk.

① Cross the bridge, noting the tiny toll booth. I am told that this was placed here for the purpose of enforcing a toll of six shillings and eightpence per time for transporting millstones over the bridge. Across the bridge, continue straight over the road and into a narrow, half-concealed passageway leading out to the fields.

Continue ahead, doubling right and left with the field boundary at one point. On entering a further L-shaped field, bear left over the field to reach a stile, beside a gate in the far corner. Join Wheatlands Lane and turn right.

② At the top of the hill, follow the road round to a stile on the right and join the waymarked path leading into the woods. A lovely woodland path follows the ridge, with wide views to right and left; across the Derwent valley on the one hand and towards Longstone Edge and Monsal Head on the other. Cross a stile on the right, descending with the path to Bramley Lane.

③ Turn left onto Bramley Lane and immediately right again, resuming the waymarked woodland route. As you proceed, the village of Calver comes into view below and to the left. After passing through an area rich in rhododendrons, the woodland is left for a spell as the path descends towards Calver.

④ Re-entering the woods, turn sharp

Bramley Lane

right at a short waymarking post; cross a stile and turn left. The path bears away from the woods as directed by the guidepost. In the next field, turn right over the stile and cross this field from corner to corner. Continue round, keeping to the right of Bramley Farm, to rejoin Bramley Lane.

⑤ Turn left, following the lane, via Bubnell hamlet, back to Baslow.

PLACES OF INTEREST NEARBY

Edensor, just to the south-west of Baslow, is the estate village of the Chatsworth estate and well worth a visit. It was specially built to replace the original village which obstructed the view from the 'Big House'. There is a fascinating variety of building styles and a beautiful landmark in the slender church spire.

Litton
The Red Lion

MAP: OUTDOOR LEISURE 24 (WHITE PEAK) (GR 164752)	WALK 17	DISTANCE: 3 MILES

DIRECTIONS TO START: FROM THE A623 (CHESTERFIELD TO CHAPEL-EN-LE-FRITH ROAD) TURN SOUTH ONTO AN UNCLASSIFIED ROAD WEST OF WARDLOW MIRES. **PARKING:** ROADSIDE, AROUND THE VILLAGE GREEN.

A pleasant upland village, with the village stocks still standing on the green, Litton was the birthplace of William Bagshawe, the Apostle of the Peak. A nonconformist minister, Bagshawe was ejected from his living at the time of the Restoration, and set up as a freelance minister, preaching throughout the wilder parts of the Peak District.

This is a nice easy stroll, first along the rim, and then in the depths, of Cressbrook Dale, with its gruesome reminder of a vicious 19th century murder.

The Red Lion

A busy and popular 17th century free house overlooking Litton's village green, the Red Lion is a grade II listed building with three open fireplaces and a cheerful atmosphere. Families with well-behaved children are welcome, likewise well-behaved dogs. Food, including daily specials, is served every lunchtime from 12 noon until 2 pm and in the evening, Monday to Saturday, between 6 pm and 8.30 pm. The inn serves traditional and guest beers and the opening hours are from 11 am until 2 pm and 6 pm to 11 pm on Monday to Friday and all day on Saturday and Sunday. Telephone 01298 871458.

The Walk

① Follow Mires Lane east out of the village. With Cressbrook Dale below on your right, cross a stile and enter the Cressbrook Dale Nature Reserve. Follow the green wallside path till you reach a step-stile on your left; cross and, over the next field, rejoin the dale-edge path, continuing to the A623 road.

② Turn right along the road. At the

Litton

Red Campion

junction with the B6465, turn sharp right along a farm lane, entering Cressbrook Dale proper, and continue to Peter's Stone, an immense limestone outcrop dominating the dale. Following a brutal murder on New Year's Day in 1815, the body of the murderer, 21-year-old Anthony Lingard, was hung in chains on Peter's Stone as a warning to others. A narrow path around the back of the rock provides, for the lithe and nimble, access to the summit.

③ Continue through the dale. On reaching a set of redundant stepping stones (or the redundant piers of an extinct footbridge?) cross the adjacent stile and enter Tansley Dale, following the path up through the dale.

④ At the head of the dale, cross a stile, bearing right over the fields. Go left along an intervening lane for a short distance only, then right again, over one more field, to Litton village.

PLACES OF INTEREST NEARBY

Tideswell, a sizeable village high on the limestone uplands at a junction of ancient ways, was, in the Middle Ages, a bustling market town and an administrative centre of some importance. It still shows, in the layout of its streets and lanes, the field pattern – and its magnificent village church, known as the Cathedral of the Peak, should not be missed.

Froggatt
The Chequers Inn

MAP: OUTDOOR LEISURE 24 (WHITE PEAK) (GR 247761)

WALK 18

DISTANCE: 3½ MILES

DIRECTIONS TO START: APPROACHING FROM CHESTERFIELD ON THE A619 (BASLOW) ROAD, TURN RIGHT AT THE CUTTHORPE TURNING AND LEFT AGAIN AT THE NEXT JUNCTION, BEARING RIGHT AT A FORK AND CONTINUING FOR 3 TO 4 MILES TO CURBAR GAP. **PARKING:** CURBAR GAP CAR PARK (GR 262747).

A particularly distinctive feature of the Peak District is the 'Edges': a chain of gritstone cliffs to the east of the River Derwent, extending from north of the Derwent and Howden Reservoirs down to the fringes of Darley Dale in the south. At the northern end they are wildly beautiful and remote, providing the enthusiast with challenging but rewarding walking. To the south, they tail away somewhat tamely around Harland and Fallinge. The most popular area is in the centre, providing miles of easy strolling over gentle, well-trodden footpaths with magnificent views across the Derwent valley – and some exciting and challenging exercise for the rock-gymnasts.

This gentle saunter along one of the finest and most popular of the Edges is followed by a descent to the welcoming arms of the Chequers. An easy riverside walk follows, the whole exercise culminating in a brief and relatively easy climb, back to Curbar Gap car park.

The Chequers Inn

A traditional coaching inn on the scenic Froggatt Edge road, the earliest records are of a row of six cottages standing on the site as long ago as 1591, these being converted into an alehouse in 1632. The inn, appropriately, has had something of a chequered history with body-snatchers, in the course of their rounds, counted among the former regulars. One or two of the old-timers appear to have lingered on, including, so the landlord tells me, the occasional Roman soldier, straying off the Curbar Gap road.

Although situated away from the residential area of nearby Froggatt village the pub is busy and popular, attracting a steady clientele of walkers, climbers and tourists. Monday to Friday opening is from 11 am to 3 pm and between 5.30 pm and 11 pm, with all-day opening at the weekends. Food is served in the week from noon until 2 pm and 6 pm until 9.30 pm, and all through the day at the weekend until 9.30 pm (9 pm on Sundays). There is an appetizing selection of full meals and bar snacks on the menu, plus a range of daily specials on the bar blackboard. Telephone 01433 630231.

The Walk

① Starting from Curbar Gap car park, follow the enclosed gravel path onto Curbar Edge. The obvious route to take is the broad, clear and well-trodden way, but a more satisfying and rewarding option, with better views, meanders around the rocky perimeter of the moor, overlooking the Derwent valley.

② A good mile on along the edge, a path leads off to the left (look for a short post with a yellow arrow waymark), leading down by a prominent rock-face. Follow this round onto the balcony below the rock-face. Look out again, carefully here, for a descending woodland path, which may not be immediately obvious. The path is initially rough, steep and stony, but safe enough – and it soon improves. Cross a stile and descend to the road, turning right a little to reach the Chequers.

③ Return along the road to the same path; cross the road and continue over a stile, descending over an open grassy area to reach a minor road and turn right. A little way on, cross a step-stile on the left and join the riverside (River Derwent) path, continuing to New Bridge.

④ Cross the road and continue, bearing left beyond the weir, up the bank and over the ensuing field. Turn right at the road, keeping left at the junction (Riddings Lane). Go left again at The Green in Curbar, by the well, and continue round to Bar Lane, turning left again here.

Below Curbar Gap

⑤ Where the road bends left, keep straight ahead through the squeezer, following the wall-side field path. Continue over the fields to rejoin the road and turn right, back to the car park.

PLACES OF INTEREST NEARBY
Grindleford Station, north-west of Froggatt (GR 250788) is the gateway to a charming walk through the wooded Padley Gorge. Padley chapel, nearby, occupies the gatehouse – all that remains of the 15th century Padley Hall where, over 400 years ago, the Catholic priests Nicholas Garlick and Robert Ludlam were arrested.

Bretton
The Barrel Inn

MAP: OUTDOOR LEISURE 24
(WHITE PEAK) (GR 201779)

WALK 19

DISTANCE: 3½ MILES (OR 1½ MILES)

DIRECTIONS TO START: VIA THE A623 (CHESTERFIELD TO CHAPEL-EN-LE-FRITH ROAD) AS FAR AS HOUSLEY, TURNING OFF HERE FOR FOOLOW AND CONTINUING NORTH UP STEEP AND NARROW BRADSHAW LANE. THE BARREL IS SITUATED AT THE HIGHEST POINT. **PARKING:** LIMITED. IF THE PUB'S OWN SPACE IS FULL, IT WILL BE NECESSARY TO PARK NEARBY ON THE GRASS VERGE.

Bretton is a tiny hamlet consisting of little more than an excellent pub and an equally desirable, traditional (ie, simple and unpretentious) Youth Hostel. Standing on the hilltop boundary between the limestone of the White Peak and the grit of the Park, there are stunning views in either direction. The story is told of a former local miner who made a bet that he could wheel a one-ton barrow load of lead ore. He won his bet; then went home and died.

One of the most delightful and popular walks in the Peak District leads down to charming Stoke Ford, and is followed by a long, but never tedious, climb back out of the valley. There is pleasure at every point, with oak woodland, grassy paths, derelict farmsteads, burbling brooks – and glorious views. Those preferring a gentler walk (but still offering excellent views) can opt for a shorter, 1½ mile road walking version.

The Barrel Inn

Dating back to the late 16th century, the Barrel is a busy and popular country pub, with claims to being the highest pub in Derbyshire and the third highest in England, and to offer views over five counties. The former local trades of smallholding and lead-mining have both now disappeared, and the pub must rely heavily on tourism – and its own excellent reputation.

Service is pleasant and obliging and the menu impressive. Specialities of the house include Cooperman's Pie, containing pork, gammon, chicken and beef, with red wine and mushroom sauce, and home-made Steak and Ale Pie. The set menu is complemented by an extensive specials board and there is a mouthwatering selection of sandwiches and snacks for those of simpler tastes.

Opening hours are from 11 am to 3 pm and 6 pm to 11 pm on Monday to Friday, with all-day opening on Saturday and Sunday. Telephone: 01433 630856.

The Walk

Note: Those wishing to take the shorter route (which can also be followed, with care, by those with baby buggies) should continue along the road from point 2 to rejoin the road leading to the Barrel and turn right.

① Take the narrow road to the left of the Barrel, passing the Youth Hostel and descending gently as you enjoy the beautiful valley view ahead.

② After about ¼ mile, the road bends rightward. Keep straight forward here, following the guideposted footpath route between walls. Cross a stile and descend easily via a lovely green path, making for Bretton Clough. By a second seat, turn sharp right with the path, descending more steeply now over stonier, wetter ground. After you cross a streamlet, a stretch of more open ground follows.

③ Where the path branches, keep straight ahead, below and to the left of a ruined farmstead, and re-enter the clough. Descend gently to Stoke Ford, a popular picnic spot for generations of ramblers. Three cloughs meet here: Bretton, Highlow and Abney. There is a little footbridge, beneath which Bretton Brook passes to join that from Abney, continuing east as Highlow Brook.

④ Retrace your steps for a short distance only, soon branching left with the path to climb steeply out of the clough. The gradient eases a little as the path veers right. Take the opportunity here to look back and admire the view. The hill across the valley to the left is Abney Low; that to the right is Highlow Hill, beyond which

The path near Bretton

following the wall, to Gotherage Plantation. Bear right over a step-stile and continue, still with the wallside green way, feeding into a farm track. Arrive at a crossways, entered via a ladder-stile.

⑥ Cross the stile and continue ahead along a rough lane, turning right at the end, back to the Barrel.

can be seen the prominent barrier of Stanage Edge, with Higger Tor and Carl Wark to its right. Continue along a green track beside the wall, bending left over a side valley and still climbing.

⑤ Cross a stile and continue, still

PLACES OF INTEREST NEARBY

The village of **Eyam**, south-east of Bretton, achieved an unsought but lasting place in history when it was struck, in 1665, by an outbreak of plague, brought to the village in a consignment of clothing carried from London. In the course of the ensuing months, 259 of the local inhabitants, out of a total population of 350, died of the infection. That the disease was confined within the village was largely due, perhaps, to the policy of isolation instituted by the rector, William Mompesson, whose own wife died in the outbreak. The plague is still remembered in the names of places in and around the village: Plague Cottages, Riley Graves, Mompesson's Well and Cucklet Dell, where open-air services were held during the infection. A sad footnote to the story – when, two or three years later, Mompesson was transferred to a Nottinghamshire parish the villagers, afraid of catching the infection, treated him as an outcast.

Longshaw
The Fox House

| MAP: OUTDOOR LEISURE 1 (DARK PEAK) AND 24 (WHITE PEAK) (GR 266803) | **WALK 20** | DISTANCE: 2 MILES |

DIRECTIONS TO START: THE PUB IS ON THE A625 (SHEFFIELD TO HATHERSAGE ROAD) OPPOSITE THE JUNCTION WITH THE B6055. **PARKING:** AT THE FOX HOUSE.

The Longshaw Estate, now in the care of the National Trust, is centred around Longshaw Lodge, once the Duke of Rutland's shooting lodge. His Grace must have entertained some impressive shooting parties in his time, because the Lodge itself is no small beer, yet the accommodation is said to have overflowed, at times, into the Fox House. In my own youth, the Lodge served a term as a Holiday Fellowship Guest House. The grounds are extensive and beautiful, providing a perfect setting for an easy 2-mile stroll that should satisfy anyone's taste. Short and sweet, with beauty and interest at every turn, there is no climbing of any significance and the paths are easy, negotiable even, with care, by baby buggies.

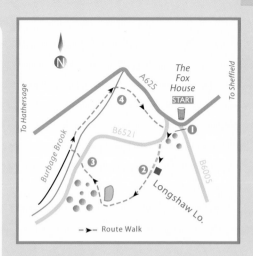

The Fox House

This impressive 18th century coaching inn owes its name, not to Wily Reynard, but to the builder of the original two-roomed cottage: one George Fox of Callow Farm. Much bigger now, the Fox House has long provided rest and refreshment to patrons of every class and condition. The annual Longshaw Sheepdog Trials, still held each September, originated here at the Fox House.

Owned by Bass Vintage Inns, the opening hours are from 11 am to 11 pm on Monday to Saturday and 12 noon until 10.30 pm on Sundays. Food is served daily from noon until one hour before closing. Specialities of the house include rump steak, caesar salad and Brie and broccoli parcels, and Fuller's London Pride cask ale is 'guested'. Overnight accommodation can be provided too. Telephone: 01433 630374.

The Walk

① Follow the road towards Hathersage, turning left onto the B6521 (Grindleford) road. Bear left by the Lodge gates, entering the Longshaw Estate and following the drive as far as the house. There is an information centre, shop and restaurant here.

Burbage Brook

The Lake, Longshaw

② Branch right opposite the Lodge, following the footpath beside the fence. Continue through a gate and round to the right, following the ditch and passing through an area of rhododendrons, and on beside an attractive small lake.

③ Cross the Grindleford road and descend to Burbage Brook; cross the footbridge and turn right. Follow the brook – a popular picnic area with super views to Carl Wark and Higger Tor – upstream as far as the next footbridge.

④ Cross the bridge and ascend the paved pathway. Where the path branches, keep right and continue back to the Grindleford road, close to the Lodge gates. Turn left here, then right again, back to Fox House.

PLACES OF INTEREST NEARBY
Longshaw Visitor Centre – admission free. For opening hours, telephone: 01433 631708. There is all year round access to the parkland.

Hathersage
The Plough

MAP: OUTDOOR LEISURE 1 (DARK PEAK)
(GR 234805)

WALK 21

DISTANCE: 3½ MILES

DIRECTIONS TO START: THE PUB IS ON THE B6001 (GRINDLEFORD) ROAD BY LEADMILL
BRIDGE, SOUTH OF HATHERSAGE. **PARKING:** AT THE PLOUGH.

A grave in Hathersage churchyard is reputed to be that of Little John. A little more recently than Robin Hood's time, Charlotte Brontë is believed to have received the inspiration for her novel *Jane Eyre* in this area. The Hope Valley history of the Eyre family dates back to the Middle Ages, when the clan were hereditary wardens – or Eyrs – of the Peak Forest. It is said that one member of the family had a house built for each of his sons, all visible from his own home.

And the halls at North Lees, Shatton, Offerton and Highlow – and the remains at Padley – all boasting connections with the Eyre dynasty, are still to be seen. Descendants of the family are still to be found, dwelling in the Hope Valley.

There are two elements to this pleasant walk. The climb up by field path and quiet lane to Offerton Hall is followed, after the descent to the River Derwent, by a gentle riverside stroll back to Leadmill Bridge.

The Plough

A free house of considerable charm, the Plough occupies an attractive position outside the town of Hathersage on the road to Grindleford. There is a separate restaurant area and the service, both here and in the lounge bar, is prompt and efficient, as befits a house on the Les Routieres list. Guest beers are available, and there is all-day opening, from 11.30 in the morning until 11 at night, in the week, and noon until 10.30 pm on Sundays. Bar food is available every lunchtime and evening; the menu is impressive and mouthwatering, and families are welcome. But patrons are asked to leave their dogs outside. Telephone: 01433 650319.

The Walk

① Follow Hathersage Road back as far as Leadmill Bridge, passing through the squeezer on the nearside, left of the bridge, and following the riverside path. After passing a derelict barn, bear left against a stile, leaving the river and ascending a steep

Offerton Hall

Stepping stones over the River Derwent

bank. Cross a step-stile and turn right, following the edge of the field and continuing ahead to reach a farm lane at Mount Pleasant.

② Turn right along the Broadhay Farm track. Leave this one after a while via a waymarked footpath on the left, passing through the gate and crossing the field on the line of the overhead wires, with woods on either side. Continue through Callow Wood – very pleasant – bearing right at a junction of paths, now climbing steeply. After emerging from the wood, turn left, ascending to Callow Farm. In the yard area, turn briefly left and arrive at a stile on your right.

③ Follow a narrow footpath over lightly wooded bracken slopes to reach a road. Turn right here, and continue to Offerton Hall, one of the ancient homes of the ubiquitous Eyres.

④ Follow the road round by the buildings, continuing on as though for the river. After passing the last house, go through a gate on the right as directed by the footpath guidepost. Descend by a clear footpath to reach the riverside, where you will find (but not use!) a stepping stone crossing.

⑤ Turn right, following the riverside path back to Leadmill Bridge. A very gentle and pleasant path this, but some care is advised where the route hugs the edge of the bank, with a wire fence on one side and a steep (and wet!) drop on the other.

PLACES OF INTEREST NEARBY
Hathersage churchyard – with the grave of Little John. Also, near Leadmill Bridge, note the circular cutlery factory building of David Mellor, voted joint thirty-seventh in a 1999 popularity poll of 20th century buildings.

Bamford
The Anglers Rest

MAP: OUTDOOR LEISURE 1 (DARK PEAK) (GR 208837)	WALK 22	DISTANCE: 3 MILES

DIRECTIONS TO START: TURN OFF THE A625 WEST OF HATHERSAGE AND GO NORTH ON THE A6013 TO BAMFORD. **PARKING:** AT THE ANGLERS REST BUT PLEASE SEEK PERMISSION FROM THE LANDLORD BEFORE LEAVING YOUR CAR WHILST YOU WALK.

Bamford is a relatively unassuming, yet attractive place which is passed through by the hordes en route for more celebrated honeypots, such as the Snake Pass and the Upper Derwent reservoirs. It lies among high hills and has three churches, three pubs, a school, a post office and a railway station. And a Roman road passed this way, as did also the packhorse men of more recent years. How many settlements of such small size can boast as much?

On our route a steep initial climb is rewarded with magnificent views, and succeeded by easy walking on gentle footpaths and ancient trackways.

The Anglers Rest

A most attractive building (and, way back, the writer's very first High Peak Sunday Lunch venue!) the Anglers Rest is, by local standards, pretty new. A Marstons house, it was built in 1876, and provides a welcoming atmosphere, with fine, hand-pulled ales and traditional home-cooked quality food. Families are welcome and there is a special children's menu. The opening hours are from 12 noon until 3 pm and 6 pm till 11 pm on Monday to Friday and there is all-day opening on Saturday and Sunday. Food is provided from noon until 3 pm and 6 pm till 9 pm in the week, and all day on Sunday. Telephone: 01433 651424.

THE Walk

① Follow Tagg's Knoll back from the Anglers Rest, turning left at the crossroads into Bamford Clough. Bear right by a white-gated entrance, now following a rough trackway. Climb steeply, pausing from time to time 'to admire the scenery' – a couple of seats by the wayside will lend encouragement. The gradient easing, the way passes through a wood to emerge onto a road.

② Turn right. Over the rise, with impressive views opening up in every direction, the road descends to cross the head of Hurst Clough, before reascending. At a guidepost on the right, cross the adjacent stile and follow the footpath beside a wood. On reaching another guidepost turn right, follow the waymarked 'Gatehouse' route over a stile and down the field. The way goes directly down the field,

PLACES OF INTEREST NEARBY

The Upper Derwent. There are three reservoirs on the Upper Derwent, of which the best known is Ladybower – reached by following the A6013 from Bamford. Opened in 1945, two villages – Derwent and Ashopton – were drowned in Ladybower's construction, and the remains of Derwent village still surface in times of drought. The two higher, and much older reservoirs are Derwent and Howden. Those wishing to visit the dams may park at Fairholmes, by Derwent Dam. Fairholmes is reached via a minor road leading off the north side of the A57 road, at the western end of the Ashopton Viaduct, and following the side of the Ladybower reservoir.

Not far from Fairholmes, close to Derwent Dam is a monument to a dog called Tip. Joseph Tagg was a shepherd who lived, before the time of the Ladybower Reservoir, at Derwent village, and who knew the local hills and moors intimately. In December 1953, he set out from his retirement home at Yorkshire Bridge, to revisit his old haunts. He never returned. Tagg's body was found, 15 weeks later, high on the Bleaklow Moors. Tip, his eleven-year-old bitch, was a short distance away, feeble and emaciated but still alive, having remained with her master throughout that bitter winter. The memorial was erected by public subscription.

A snowy approach to nearby Win Hill

to the left of a big house; do not be misled by the sheep track, more to the left. In a further field, follow the cloughlet to a stile and join a narrow lane, turning right.

③ Follow the road (Hurstclough Lane), bearing right by a seat, where the way deteriorates to a rough stony lane – noting, as you proceed, the occasional gritstone paving. This insignificant-seeming lane is, in fact, very ancient, having formed, at one time, a section of the Roman Long Causeway road between Brough and Templeborough. The paving is almost certainly more recent, probably dating from the days of the packhorse trains. The track has evidently been overlaid at some stage, but erosion of the later surface has revealed sufficient of the paving to endorse the antiquity of the road.

④ At a guidepost on the right, descend the steps to cross the brook via a footbridge; climb the stile and continue through the wood, ascending a 'ladder' of many steps (I counted a hundred and twelve). Join a metalled roadway, following the perimeter fence of the Bamford Filters. Cross an access road and continue along the waymarked footpath route, still following the boundary fence, and turning right onto a second access road.

⑤ Bear left at a junction and leave the road via a kissing gate on the left. Cross the wood, turning left down the ensuing field to reach Joan Lane. Turn right, back to Bamford and the Anglers Rest.

Hope
The Cheshire Cheese

DIRECTIONS TO START: THE A625 (SHEFFIELD TO CHAPEL-EN-LE-FRITH ROAD) PASSES HOPE STATION, EAST OF HOPE VILLAGE. **PARKING:** HOPE STATION APPROACH ROAD (GR 180832).

The village of Hope, in the valley of the same name, sits at the foot of two popular hills with the complementary names of Lose Hill and Win Hill – reputed to have stemmed from a battle, many centuries ago, when the contending armies camped on opposing hills. The village dates back to Saxon times and was, historically, a place of some importance, more than simply the capital of

Hopedale, for the parish was one of the largest in England, occupying about two thirds of the Royal Forest of the Peak. A modest little town today, it still occupies a special place in the hearts of all Peak-wanderers.

This gentle and easy valley walk along quiet lanes and field paths culminates in a stroll beside the unassuming little River Noe.

The Cheshire Cheese

The 16th century Cheshire Cheese owes its name to its former status as an overnight stopping place on the trans-Pennine salt route, when payment for lodging was actually made in cheese; the original cheese-hooks are still be be seen. There is a relaxed old-world atmosphere here today, with open fireplaces, hand-pulled ales and good, wholesome home-prepared food. Opening hours are subject to some variation according to season, but the basic pattern is from noon until 3 pm and 6.30 pm to 11 pm on Monday to Friday. The pub is open all day on Saturday, and Sunday hours are from noon to 4 pm and 6.30 pm to 10.30 pm. Food is served daily from noon until 2.30 pm and 6.30 pm to 9 pm, with a tempting selection of full meals, bar snacks and sandwiches. Children are welcome; so also are dogs, on leads – and well-behaved adults! Overnight accom-modation is available. Telephone: 01433 620381.

The Walk

① Starting from the station car park, cross the line via the footbridge, following the path round to reach the fields. Continue with the brook on your right, heading towards Win Hill, prominent ahead. The summit, visible above the ridge, is Win Hill Pike. Turn left at Aston, following the lane round the bend and past the entrance to Birchfield Hall.

② Turn right at the entrance to Fairfield Farm, passing a bungalow and branching left by the farm. The way continues along a pleasant easy field-side track and through a wooded area. Pass beneath a railway bridge and continue to a T-junction. Turn left now, crossing Killhill Bridge over the River Noe and immediately turning right along a little footpath, to reach Edale Road. Turn right and continue to the Cheshire Cheese.

Cowslip

The countryside around Hope

③ Return to Killhill Bridge, and, having recrossed the bridge turn right along a riverside diveway. Through a farm gate reach a former mill, now converted to a residential property. Swing left between the house and the river, bearing left to find and cross a concealed site and join a field path. Follow the riverside path to the A625 road and turn left, back to Hope Station.

PLACES OF INTEREST NEARBY

North Lees Hall, near Hathersage (GR 236834) is not open to the public, but a public footpath passes the house. A square-built Elizabethan Manor house, it is believed to have been the inspiration for Charlotte Brontë's Thornfield Hall. The Jane Eyre of the story may be fiction, but there certainly was a Jane Eyre; and North Lees was one of the family residences – along with Highlow, Offerton, Shatton, Crookhill et al. The ruins can still be seen, close to North Lees, of the tiny Catholic Chapel built by Robert Eyre in 1685, but destroyed by a Protestant mob three years later.

Castleton
The Castle Inn

DIRECTIONS TO START: THE A625 FROM SHEFFIELD PASSES THROUGH CASTLETON; THE WESTERN APPROACH IS DIVERTED THROUGH THE WINNATS PASS – LIGHT VEHICLES ONLY. **PARKING:** PAY AND DISPLAY, OPPOSITE SIDE OF THE MAIN STREET FROM THE CASTLE INN.

Castleton is one of the Peak District's premier tourist traps, the castle being that built by William Peveril, natural son of the Conqueror and the one-time bailiff of the Peak Forest. Little remains of the castle today, apart from the shell of the keep, which dominates the town from the hillside above, but the main attraction these days is, perhaps, its caverns. Peak and Speedwell with their stalactites and stalagmites; Treak Cliff and Blue John with their fluorspar mining associations. This walk completes a circuit of the four main cavern systems, ending with a descent through the awesome gorge of the Winnats Pass.

The Castle Inn

The history of the Castle Inn goes back over three centuries. One early landlord in the time of Charles II was fined for brewing ale without a licence. More recently, the inn was a regular calling point on the Wellington Express coach run between Manchester and Sheffield; and four former guests were so impressed with the service that they are reported still to be in residence, in spirit at least. Great British food is served here, all day and every day, and there is an appropriate menu for every special occasion, including St George's Day and St Valentine's Day. The bar stocks 40 New World wines, two guest hand-pulled beers and eight standard beers and ales. There is a family room and a children's play area, and well-behaved dogs are welcome. Daily opening is from 11 am through to 11 pm, with food provided between 11.30 am and 10 pm. Overnight accommodation is offered too. Telephone: 01433 620578.

The Walk

① From the car park, cross the road and follow the signposted riverside walk. At a road, turn right over the bridge and continue up Goosehill. The road leads into a stony lane and thence onto a field path, following the field wall, with steep hills all around as we approach the head of the valley.

② Cross the road by the Speedwell Cavern, keeping straight forward over the field with the wall on your right, to reach a step-stile. Continue, passing to the left of a wood and climbing up to Treak Cliff

Cavern, where, apart from the cavern itself, you will find refreshments and souvenirs.

③ The way passes through the Treak Cliff site, continuing around the hillside. The path is narrow, over steep slopes, so take care. At a pair of stiles, Mam Tor comes in

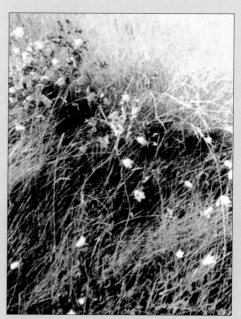

Harebells

Winnats Pass

sight, dominating the view to the right. Cross the left-hand stile and continue over level grassland to reach Blue John Cavern.

④ Past Blue John Cavern, continue up and over, to reach Winnats Pass.

⑤ Turn left, keeping to the path on the left of the wall in preference to the road. The Winnats Pass is awe-inspiring: a unique gorge with a narrow unfenced road leading down steeply into Castleton. Drivers used to use the pass purely for the experience, but since the main road over Mam Tor collapsed a few years ago, they now do so of necessity, adding to the volume of traffic through the ravine. Re-pass Speedwell Cavern, continuing via the road back to Castleton. Keep well in to the right until you reach the A625. There is no pavement, and some drivers appear to take the sign 'Speedwell' as a personal injunction!

PLACES OF INTEREST NEARBY

There is no shortage of interest here for the visitor. Apart from **Peveril Castle** (telephone: 01433 620613 for opening details), the **Village Museum** in the former Methodist Schoolroom is well worth visiting. And there are the **caverns**: Peak (01433 620285), Speedwell (01433 620512), Treak Cliff (01433 620571) and Blue John (01433 620638).

Edale
The Old Nag's Head

MAP: OUTDOOR LEISURE 1 (DARK PEAK) (GR 123860)	**WALK 25**	DISTANCE: 3¾ MILES

DIRECTIONS TO START: A625 TO HOPE. TURN NORTH BY THE CHURCH, FOLLOWING EDALE ROAD FOR 5 MILES TO THE CAR PARK, ON THE RIGHT IMMEDIATELY BEFORE EDALE VILLAGE. **PARKING:** EDALE PAY AND DISPLAY (GR 125853).

Edale is special. A lovely valley surrounded by beautiful hills, and accessible by road at only two points, via a single unclassified road. A mecca for generations of hill-walkers and bog-trotters, and the starting point of the challenging Pennine Way. Yet, for all that, there are still opportunities here for gentler, valley walking. On this particular stroll, you will find easy field paths, and no climbing of any consequence. But the hills are all around, to delight the eye without taxing the muscles. And, when you reach the end, you may still boast that you have walked a little of the Pennine Way.

The Old Nag's Head

Owned by Dorbiere Ltd, of Eccles, the Old Nag's Head is the official starting point of the 270 mile Pennine Way. Dating back to 1577, the inn claims to be one of the '100 Great Pubs of England'. On a more macabre note: the Hikers' Bar served as a mortuary during the 1939/45 war, following a plane crash in the vicinity. Opening hours are from 12 noon until 11 pm in the week and 10.30 pm on Sundays. Food is served from noon until 3 pm and 6 pm till 9 pm on Monday to Friday and all day on Saturday and Sunday until 9 pm and 8 pm respectively. There is the usual range of traditional meals, bar snacks and sandwiches, including sea food and vegetarian dishes, plus the Nag's Head Special of Yorkshire pudding filled with rich stew and added chips, and the Hiker's Special – Cornish pasty and jumbo sausage. Overnight accommodation is also available. Telephone: 01433 670291.

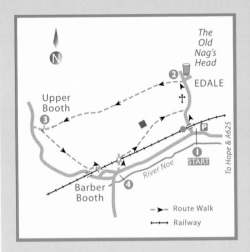

The Walk

① Starting from the car park, follow the village street through to the Old Nag's Head, at the top of the village.

② To the left of the road, opposite the pub, turn left by the four-way guidepost, following the route indicated for Upper Booth and the Pennine Way. A trenched way beneath overhanging trees, the old

The Vale of Edale

Peat Lane

Peat Lane along which the peat used to be brought down from the moor on sleds, leads up to a bridle gate and thence, via a stile on the left, to open fields. A clear path, much of it paved, climbs gently over the fields towards the head of the valley, before descending again to the hamlet of Upper Booth.

③ On the approach to Upper Booth Farm the way branches: one way continuing through the farmyard, the other turning left through a gate, for Barber Booth. Take this second route, forsaking the Pennine Way route (but take heart; you are now only 269 miles from Kirk Yetholm!). The path is less clear than the previous one, but the line is still recognisable over the grass of the fields. The path eventually merges with a farm track, turning right over the railway and through a farmyard to reach Barber Booth village.

④ Follow the village road through, bearing left just short of the Edale road onto a farm track, and recrossing the railway. Turn right through a gate and join a field path, continuing along the clear line of the path as far as Shaw Wood. Cross the farm drive and over a stile, taking the right-hand path. Across this field and another stile, continue beside the hedge-line back to Edale village. Turn right for the car park.

PLACES OF INTEREST NEARBY
Mam Tor, south of Edale village, is known as the Shivering Mountain on account of its crumbling, shaly southern face. The site of a Bronze Age hill fort, access is not difficult. There is a public car park at Mam Gap, from where a well-paved stairway leads up to the summit.

Hayfield
The Sportsman

<table>
<tr><td>MAP: OUTDOOR LEISURE 1 (DARK PEAK)
(GR 044867)</td><td>WALK 26</td><td>DISTANCE: 3¼ MILES</td></tr>
</table>

DIRECTIONS TO START: HAYFIELD IS JUST OFF THE A624, THE CHAPEL-EN-LE-FRITH TO GLOSSOP ROAD. LEAVE THE TOWN CENTRE VIA BANK STREET AND KINDER ROAD, PASSING THE SPORTSMAN INN AND CONTINUING FOR ABOUT ½ MILE TO THE CAR PARK. **PARKING:** BOWDEN BRIDGE (PAY AND DISPLAY, GR 049870).

Hayfield has, for many years, been one of the traditional meccas for those seeking to refresh their spirit in the wildness of the High Peak. The railway – which used to play host at weekends to thousands of Manchester ramblers – has been closed for many years and is now, like its Tissington counterpart, a recreational trail. But you cannot deny history. It was here, in the early 1930s, that the Kinder trespass began; still regarded by many as a significant landmark in the campaign for access to the northern moorlands.

This walk will serve as an introduction to the highest 'peak' in the Peak District, and to one of the area's classic walks. But there is no call for panic. Apart from one short, steepish ascent along the way, it is all easy going, with grand views to inspire the novice to greater heights.

The Sportsman

A Thwaites house, the Sportsman nestles at the foot of Kinder Scout, the highest mountain in the Peak District. Hand-pulled beers are served here in the traditional bar, before log fires in winter, and overnight accommodation is available for those seeking a relaxing break in beautiful surroundings. Opening hours are from noon until 3 pm daily, except Monday, and 7 pm until 11 pm (10.30 pm on Sunday) in the evening. Fine home-made food is served every lunchtime, except Monday, from 12 noon until 2 pm and in the evening, except Sunday, from 7 pm until 9 pm. The printed menu is supplemented with daily blackboard specials and there is a traditional roast on Sundays, for which bookings are recommended. Telephone: 01663 741565.

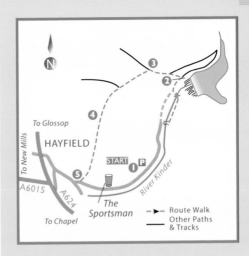

The Walk

① The walk begins at the Bowden Bridge car park, which occupies the site of the former stone quarry from which, on 24 April 1932, the mass trespass of Kinder Scout commenced. Turn left out of the car park, following the guidepost directions as for William Clough, with the River Kinder on your right. Cross a bridge beside a gated entrance, bearing left then onto the waymarked riverside footpath. Recross the river via a footbridge, turning right to arrive at the Water Authority access gates. Pass through the bridle gates on the left, and ascend the steeply paved pathway to the top of the Kinder Dam. A lovely spot this, with Kinder Reservoir nestling in a hollow of high hills. The Kinder massif provides a bulk backdrop, with the lesser summits of

South Head and Mount Famine prominent to the right.

② Turn sharp left at a junction of paths, still climbing, beside a wall. Pass through a gap in the wall ahead and join the Snake Path, at White Brow. The Snake Path forms a part of one of the Peak District's finest walks – the Kinder round, which completely encircles Kinder Scout. Not a walk for novices, the total distance of over 20 miles includes some of the wildest and remotest terrain in the area. Needless to say, the section we are following is one of the gentler bits!

③ Bear left at a junction of paths, crossing a peaty area and passing to the left of a white shooting cabin. Follow a gently undulating track over the moor. Bearing left again at another parting of the ways, keeping to the Snake Path bridleway and continuing through a gate.

④ Through a second gate bear right, descending easily over pleasant field paths with a good view over Hayfield, to reach

The Snake Path

Kinder Road. A notice near the bottom of the path records the restoration, in 1990, of a series of metal kissing-gates negotiated along the way and forming part of the Snake route.

⑤ Turn left along Kinder Road for the Sportsman, continuing on from there for the car park.

PLACES OF INTEREST NEARBY

The town of **New Mills**, to the west of Hayfield along the A6015, has much to interest the visitor. Particularly recommended is the **Torrs Riverside Park**, a stupendous gorge where two rivers combine amid a maze of bridges and viaducts. You can, of course, drive to New Mills. But why not walk there via the Sett Valley Trail from Hayfield – it isn't far.

Low Bradfield
The Plough

MAP: OUTDOOR LEISURE 1 (DARK PEAK) (GR 263916)

WALK 27

DISTANCE: 3¼ MILES

DIRECTIONS TO START: FOLLOW THE A61 AND A6101 FROM SHEFFIELD TO MALIN BRIDGE; THENCE VIA THE B6077 TO STACEY BANK, CONTINUING BESIDE DAMFLASK RESERVOIR TO HIGH AND LOW BRADFIELD. **PARKING:** THE SANDS, AT THE WESTERN END OF LOW BRADFIELD (GR 262920).

The area to the immediate west of Sheffield is a small paradise, which compares favourably with any of the more familiar honeypots of the Peak District. Sheffield's own 'Little Lakeland', it is dotted with attractive reservoirs nestling in gorgeous wooded hills. Peaceful today, it was not always so. In 1864, the newly completed Dale Dike Dam burst, bringing death and devastation to the Loxley valley and Sheffield, and beyond. In all, 244 people died in the flood, and some 20,000 were rendered homeless.

A straightforward circuit of Agden Reservoir, this walk offers easy walking all the way and no significant climbing and no stiles to negotiate. The route is not impossible with wheelchairs, provided one is prepared to tolerate some unevenness of ground and a short narrow stretch of footpath at one point.

The Plough

The frankly plain exterior of the Plough (its full title is the Plough Inn and Barn Restaurant) is belied by its relaxing and friendly interior environment. The bar area is bright and attractive with old beams, brassware and bier-steins; and heraldic escutcheons decorate the face of the bar counter. Traditional country fare is on offer here from 11.30 am to 2.30 pm in the week and 12 noon until 2 pm on Sundays, also every evening from 7 pm until 10 pm. Specialities of the house include a business lunch, a Saturday carvery, traditional Sunday lunch – and take-away fish and chips. Opening hours are from 11.30 am to 4 pm and 6.30 pm until 11 pm in the week, 12 noon till 4 pm and 7 pm to 10.30 pm on Sundays. Telephone: 0114 2851280.

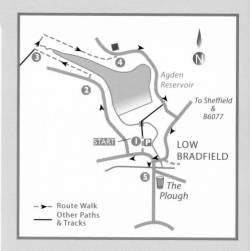

The Walk

① Start from the public car park. Follow The Sands to Fair House Lane and turn right; then right again at Windy Bank. Follow the road past a lodge house and alongside Agden Reservoir.

Agden Reservoir

Low Bradfield

② Leave the road via a waymarked footpath (described as an Easy Going Trail) on the right, following a beautiful woodland lane.

③ Bear right with the track, crossing Emlin Dike and Agden Dike and continuing, now on the opposite side of the reservoir. Join the road by Smallfield Cottage (big cottage, no field!) and turn right.

④ The road is followed from here to the Plough, turning right at a T-junction and following the road round and over a stone bridge. There is a pretty picnic spot here, complete with ducks on the brook. Turn left for the pub.

⑤ Return to the bridge, but do not cross it. Continue straight ahead, back to The Sands and the car park.

Note: Those not wishing to visit the pub en route are recommended to leave the road soon after passing Agden Dam, following an enclosed footpath beside a bungalow on the right. Not suitable for wheelchairs, this leads down a delightful stepped path and over a footbridge, back to The Sands – may be muddy towards the end.

PLACES OF INTEREST NEARBY
While in the Bradfield area, why not take time to explore the nearby **Rivelin and Loxley valleys**: access respectively via the A57/A6101 and B6077 roads? Local tradition identifies Loxley as the birthplace of Robin Hood.

Langsett
The Waggon and Horses

DIRECTIONS TO START: LANGSETT IS ON THE A616, SOUTH OF HUDDERSFIELD AND WEST OF JUNCTION 35A OF THE M1. **PARKING:** LANGSETT BARN PUBLIC CAR PARK (GR 211004) – SEE NOTE AT THE PUB DETAILS.

Langsett is no more than a hamlet, on the busy main road between Sheffield and Huddersfield, close to its junction with the A628 Barnsley to Manchester road. But do not underestimate the place. It stands on the very perimeter of the Peak District, the gateway to some of the bleakest, yet most inspiring, of Peak District country. It has a good family pub, a Youth Hostel – and an attractive reservoir.

And one of the finest walks in the district, the ancient Cut Gate route to the Derwent valley, starts from here. This walk isn't the Cut Gate, but it briefly covers some of the same ground. Basically a circuit of the reservoir, it combines delightful woodland paths with safe and easy moorland walking. And the whole route is along clear, well-marked paths, lanes and tracks.

The Waggon and Horses

This is a well-established family operated free house offering prompt and friendly service. The facilities include an outside drinking area and a non-smoking area, and families are welcome, as also are well-behaved dogs. The opening hours are from noon until 3 pm and 7 pm till 11 pm in the week; lunchtime only on Sundays, from noon until 3 pm, or 4 pm in summer. Food is available daily from noon until 2 pm (on Sundays, traditional lunch only) and from 7 pm until 9 pm between Tuesday and Saturday. A particular favourite is the home-made meat and potato pie, with mushy peas and red cabbage – and bilberry pie to follow! Telephone: 01226 763147.

For the convenience of potential passing trade, those taking the walk are respectfully asked not to leave their cars in the limited space provided by the pub car park while doing so, but to use instead the Langsett Barn car park, which is close at hand.

The Walk

① Starting from the Langsett Barn car park, follow the gravelled path through the car park, and a hand-gate, continuing on beside the woodland along the waymarked circular route. There are tantalising glimpses through the trees of the Langsett Reservoir, below on the left.

② Shortly after passing a stepped footpath on your right, turn left at a T-junction (with multiple waymarks), descending to cross the reservoir's feeder river, which rejoices in a choice of names: The Porter or Little Don. Turn left with

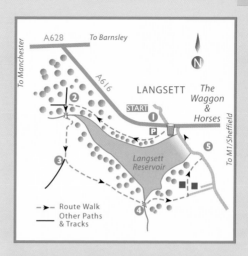

the path, winding right and left onto Hingcliff Common. This route leads to Cut Gate and, eventually, to the Howden, Derwent and Ladybower Reservoirs – a very long walk with no shelter. But do not panic, that is reserved for another occasion!

Forget-me-nots

Woodland skirting Langsett Reservoir

③ Turn left at a guidepost, as directed by the circular walk waymark. A clear broad track leads over the moor, giving excellent views of the reservoir. Pass the ruins of North America Farm – a long derelict victim of the reservoir builders? – and continue ahead, again following the woodland edge.

④ Cross Thickwoods Brook and, after a brief flirtation with the reservoir, re-enter the woods. Follow the succeeding lane to a junction and turn left, now following a waymarked green track. Left again at the buildings and right at a public footpath sign, to reach the road.

⑤ Turn left and follow the road over the reservoir dam, back to Langsett. Turn left for the Waggon and Horses, and the car park.

PLACES OF INTEREST NEARBY

A wild and wandering motor tour of the 'Sheffield Highlands' leaves Langsett via the minor road to Langsett and Midhope reservoirs. The possibilities are unlimited and include the Ewden valley.

Holme
The Fleece

MAP: OUTDOOR LEISURE 1 (DARK PEAK) (GR 108059)

WALK 29

DISTANCE: 2 MILES

DIRECTIONS TO START: HOLME IS ON THE A6024 SOUTH-WEST OF HOLMFIRTH.
PARKING: AT THE FLEECE, FOR PATRONS. OTHERWISE ON STREET PARKING NEARBY.

The village of Holme is the last place you come to before crossing the desolate moorland road over Holme Moss, to Woodhead and Longdendale – but not, by any means, the last place you would choose to visit! For there is beauty hereabouts, and pleasant walking, as fans of *Last of the Summer Wine* will recognise. This is the area immortalised by the long-running television series. And who knows? You might even recognise some of the spots visited on this walk; on the moorland fringe, where deep cloughs and tumbling streams alternate with the wooded shores of secluded reservoirs.

The Fleece

Well over two hundred years old, the Fleece is a supremely welcoming hostelry, recently refurbished but still traditional, high on the Pennine moors, with an open log fireplace – and extending a warm welcome to all comers. You will find good home-cooked food here, washed down, if you wish, with hand-pulled and guest beers. The regular menu is supplemented by daily blackboard specials, and a two-course luncheon, at attractive prices, is served from Tuesday to Friday. Opening hours are from 11.30 am to 2 pm and 7 pm to 9 pm on Tuesday to Saturday, with all-day opening on Sundays. The pub is closed on Mondays apart from bank holidays. Telephone: 01484 683449.

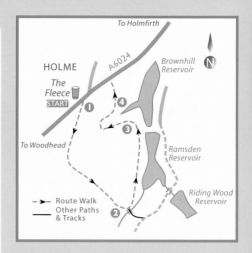

The Walk

① From the Fleece, cross the road and follow the waymarked footpath past the houses and down over the fields to Gill Hey Bridge. Cross, and ascend the steps, continuing over the moor top and beside a broken wall, before descending steeply to Netherley Clough.

Netherley Clough

Above Ramsden Reservoir

② Turn sharp left in the clough (do not cross the bridge), continuing along the concessionary path to the left of Ramsden Reservoir. This is a nice path with lovely views – but care is called for over a short distance as you ascend a narrow section of path over steeply sloping ground opposite the dam.

③ Cross a stile; then descend and cross a second, leading into woodland and bearing left with the path above a stream in an arm of Brownhill Reservoir. The path descends to cross the stream via a footbridge. Take

time here to admire the waterfall, before ascending along the opposite bank. Continue left over a field to a stile beside a wood.

④ Turn left along an enclosed footpath, following the Kirklees Way arrows to Holme village. Turn left for the Fleece.

PLACES OF INTEREST NEARBY
While in the area, why not spend an hour or two in **Holmfirth**, seeking out the haunts of Compo, Clegg and Co? Or savouring the birthplace of the 'Bamforth' saucy postcard?

Uppermill
The Cross Keys

MAP: OUTDOOR LEISURE 1 (DARK PEAK)
(GR 008063)

WALK 30

DISTANCE: 3¼ MILES

DIRECTIONS TO START: TURN EAST OFF THE A670 (MANCHESTER TO STANDEDGE)
ROAD IN THE CENTRE OF UPPERMILL, FOLLOWING THE SIGNED ROAD FOR
SADDLEWORTH CHURCH, CONTINUING FOR ONE MILE AND OVER THE CROSSROADS.
PARKING: AT THE CROSS KEYS.

The township of Uppermill, sitting on the rim of the Pennines, has on its doorstep some excellent walking country and is a particularly popular stamping ground for the ramblers of Manchester. It likewise deserves to be discovered by those from further afield.

This walk starts with a short, but not over-strenuous pull up onto the gentle moorland east of Saddleworth Fold, introducing us to the Oldham Way and taking us past the prominent war memorial by Kinder Stones. We return to the start by way of gentle paths around the lower slopes.

The Cross Keys

This fine and friendly 18th century building is situated to the rural east of Uppermill, close to the ancient parish church of Saddleworth. You will find a genuine welcome here, and real log fires in winter. And just to dispel any misgivings about the safety of the walking, the Oldham Mountain Rescue Team has its headquarters here! This is one of J. W. Lees' houses; open daily from 11 am to 11 pm (12 noon until 10.30 pm on Sundays), with a good range of locally brewed real ale and 25 years inclusion in the *Good Beer Guide* to prove it. Food is available every day from noon until 2.30 pm and 5 pm till 7 pm; noon until 7 pm on Saturday and Sunday. There is a tempting selection of main meals, fish dishes, vegetarian fare, sandwiches and children's meals. Not to mention a large beer garden and a children's play area. Families are welcome. Telephone: 01457 874626.

The Walk

① Outside the pub turn left, passing Pobgreen Lane. Turn right opposite Clerk's Cottage, crossing a stile and following the waymarked Oldham Way footpath. Initially a sunken way, this continues for a space as a walled lane, before reverting to a trenched field path, ascending steadily.

② On the rim of the moor turn right,

Shaw Rocks

Sugar Loaf

following the line of the wall above Slades Rocks. Keep to the higher ground as the path slants left away from the wall, passing close to Shaw Rocks; and, if you wish, branching left a little to take in the Sugar Loaf. Continue ahead to a crossing track and turn right, to reach the war memorial obelisk on Kinder Stones, erected in recognition of those from the Saddleworth area who gave their lives in two world wars.

③ From against the entrance to the railed enclosure, a rudimentary path descends to join and follow a dip beside a broken wall. Turn right (west) on meeting a second broken wall, following a footpath – possibly a little unclear – which hugs the hillside on your right. This path soon becomes plainer, before merging with a sunken lane which, in turn, leads out to the road by Knowl Top Farm. Turn right.

④ Past Knowl Top Farm, continue to Knowl Farm and turn right, into a flagged lane. Where the track bends left to reach a farmhouse, keep straight ahead over the stile, following a wallside footpath. Continue for about ¹/₂ mile, keeping to the wallside where it exists; elsewhere contouring along the hillside, to reach a walled green lane and the hamlet of Pobgreen. Turn left and follow Pobgreen Lane back to the Cross Keys.

PLACES OF INTEREST NEARBY
Dovestone, just off the A635 at Greenfield (Oldham), is the largest in a string of three reservoirs. Nestling in a deep hollow of rugged moorland hills, this is a delightful spot in which to park and potter around by the waterside.